PILGRIMAGE
TOWARD THE
LIGHT

MELINDA HOLCOMB

Leavitt Peak Press

ISBN: 978-1-964462-06-6 (sc)
ISBN: 978-1-964462-07-3 (e)

Rev. date: 05/02/2024

I wish to dedicate this work to my sweet husband, Randall Holcomb, who by his loving support, faithfulness, and encouragement helped me heal and helps me heal more every day.

In addition, I respectfully dedicate this work to my therapist, Raymond M. Wheeler, who stood by me through all the years of remembrance and pain with patience, longsuffering, care, and compassion. He has been my God-given guide through all the difficult years.

CONTENTS

INTRODUCTION-CONCERNING DISSOCIATIVE IDENTITY DISORDER.. V

1   TESTIMONY TO THE LIGHT 1
2   DARKNESS WILL NOT WIN 9
3   EARLY POETRY 34
4   PILGRIMS ALL... 64
5   MY SAFE PLACE 78
6   MISSION JOURNEYS...91
7   HOSPITAL TRAUMAS.. 105
8   LATER POETRY 116
9   ABBA'S HOUSE 127
10   BRAND NEW LIFE 138
11   MOVING ON... 155

EPILOGUE 165
RESOURCES 173

INTRODUCTION
Concerning Dissociative Identity Disorder

The problem of this project is the observation and evaluation of the struggle of a woman through the complexities of childhood trauma; how she survived and overcame these complexities. A background is given herein of the disorders caused by complex trauma pertinent to this testimony. I pray to assist the hurting individual, and by God's grace help with the healing.

❧ ❧

Many years ago, I was diagnosed with Post-Traumatic Stress Disorder (PTSD), Anxiety Disorder, Dissociative Identity Disorder (DID), formerly called Multiple Personality Disorder, Major Depression, and Bipolar Disorder due to traumatic abuse in childhood. Today there is much information documented on the disorders of my focus here, and help is available to a greater degree than in past generations. I was terrified when I was told that there were very real reasons that I suffered and felt "crazy," and "unreal." I did not want to believe that the events really happened to me that caused these diagnoses. When the unthinkable happens to young children, the result is much the same as for a combat veteran of war, or first responders as these groups can be affected by Post-Traumatic Stress

Disorder. Shocking sights, sounds, and terrors grip the hearts of the young and old alike. Children are sometimes better able to shut out the memories and go on with life, at least for a few years, while traumatized adults simply cannot forget the horrors they have faced. Sometimes events in childhood can be perpetrated by evil abusers and sometimes there can be accidental events that cause a person to dissociate, both of which happened to me.

Post-traumatic stress affects over 80 percent of Americans, with approximately 9 percent developing Post-Traumatic Stress Disorder. Post-traumatic stress is more common in those in law enforcement, those in disaster work, and war veterans. Though many people have post-traumatic stress reactions, not all develop the disorder.[1] Persons who do not receive help after a crisis may develop the disorder after a period of time. PTSD is common in children following abusive, stressful, and shocking events. PTSD is characterized by the lack of treatment or care, for whatever reason, of the severely stressed person. "Stress reactions are survival mechanisms in a psychological crisis. An acute response to this type of crisis happens when a person's psychological balance is disrupted, causing increased stress, when one's usual coping mechanisms have failed, and when there is evidence of significant distress, impairment, and dysfunction."[2] While post-traumatic stress is a survival mechanism, Post-Traumatic Stress Disorder is a pathogenic mechanism of those who either do not receive help or who refuse help from others. If Post-Traumatic Stress lasts longer than a month, it can be classified as the disorder.

In children who have been abused, help is usually not available except in special circumstances. Most are left to wander on alone into adulthood and then many never receive help. Some people refuse to look at the past, refuse to believe what has happened to cripple their lives, sometimes refuse to believe their lives are crippled, and

---

[1] Jitender Sareen, MD, FRCPC. *Post-traumatic Stress Disorder in Adults: Impact, Comorbidity, Risk Factors, and Treatment.* http://www.ncbi.nlm.nih.gov. Accessed 5/13/20.

[2] Jeffrey T. Mitchell PhD., C.T.S. *CISM: Group Crisis Intervention 4th Edition* (Ellicot City, MD: I.C.I.S.F., Inc., 2006), 20.

refuse to give up addictive processes such as alcohol, drugs and other addictions that are helping them temporarily cope. These people never receive emotional healing, but dysfunction is perpetuated in their families, sadly. Those who are left to wander often become severely mentally ill.[3]

There are two types of stress: eustress and distress. Eustress is good stress, or low levels of stress, which can heighten awareness in the individual and assist them in performing certain tasks more efficiently. Distress is harmful stress of high magnitude following a crisis.[4] With proper help, traumatized individuals can recover from traumatic distress. Distress, if left untreated, can become chronic, leaving individuals to live in a heightened state of crisis most all the time.[5]

Severe levels of stress can affect a person in every aspect of their being, affecting the physical, spiritual, emotional aspects, as well as the thought processes. "Physical symptoms that signify severe stress are excessive sweating, increased heart rate, rapid breathing, increased blood pressure, dizziness, and weakness to name a few."[6] Physical disease is therefore often caused by stress, as stress affects all the major body systems. Much sickness and many hospitalizations are due to physical stress on the human body.[7] Physicians agree that stress has effects that cause disease.

Thought processes can be impaired and is evidenced by several signs and symptoms as well. Anxiety is the body's response to a threat or danger perceived by the person even when there is no current danger. The person has most often had a threat of death to the self or has witnessed threats to others, whether or not the act was carried out. Later in the process of a stress disorder, the person has panic attacks for no apparent reason, even when circumstances

---

[3] Mitchell, ibid.

[4] Mental Help Online. *Types of Stressors (Eustress vs. Distress)*. http://www.mentalhelp.net. Accessed 5/13/20.

[5] Ibid.

[6] Ibid, 219.

[7] Types of Stressors, Ibid.

prove that all should be at peace within. Anxiety attacks often happen at unpredictable times, even years after the original trauma, due to flashbacks. Flashbacks are images that appear in the mind and memory for no apparent reason. Usually there is a reason for the impaired thought processes of flashbacks, though the reason may be unknown to the survivor.

Signs and symptoms of impaired thought process are as follows. "Some examples of cognitive symptoms are confusion, nightmares, hypervigilance (always looking for and feeling one is in danger; being always in "fight or flight" mode), intrusive images (or flashbacks), and poor concentration."[8] This list is not exhaustive. "Symptoms of emotional stress are fear, guilt, grief, panic, denial, anxiety, emotional shock, depression, intense anger, and emotional outbursts. Behavioral symptoms are withdrawal, erratic movements, addictions, and changes in ordinary behavior. Spiritual stress can cause anger at God, questioning basic beliefs, loss of meaning or purpose and sense of isolation from God."[9] All these symptoms and more are evident in severe stress reactions and are temporary if the person is treated properly.

In PTSD, however, more symptoms appear and linger. "Further symptoms include numbing withdrawal and avoidance, antisocial acts, repetitive, intrusive memories or recollections of the trauma and/or events related to the trauma. All symptoms have a duration of at least one month and cause significant distress and dysfunction."[10] In stress management teams, members are taught to do immediate work to provide assistance to those in crisis.

PTSD, the disorder, requires intensive counseling to heal. Healing can take many years and then it may only be better, but not fully healed. For instance, personally, though I am living a happy and healthy lifestyle, I struggled at times with flashbacks. I have had help through E.M.D.R. which is a fascinating process. The acronym

---

[8] Mitchell, Ibid.
[9] Ibid.
[10] Ibid, 33.

stands for "eye movement desensitization and reprocessing." It is difficult to imagine how it works, but I have been helped.

I am not immobilized by flashbacks now. I simply slow down, acknowledge the flashback, deal with the emotions surrounding the flashbacks, and move on. At times, the stress itself may cause the flashbacks. When I am very stressed, I know that I need to engage in de-stressing behaviors specific to me. I do not have flashbacks since having ART (Accelerated Resolution Therapy). Accelerated Resolution Therapy began as EMDR, but this new style was developed post 9/11 after the tragedies in our country. It is a very effective therapy. It is comforting and deals with traumatic images in the mind even better than EMDR in my experience. It is not hypnosis.

My specific de-stressing behaviors are taking a very warm bubble bath, watching a movie (one that does not require much thought, so that I can just be a couch potato and enjoy), and, sometimes, playing the piano. The most effective is to go camping and hiking in the mountains and the wilderness with my husband. We do the latter as often as possible. Every person will have their own de-stressing behaviors and what works for one person will not necessarily work for another.

There is much documented on Dissociative Identity Disorder, which is a common reaction to trauma that is so severe that the human mind cannot comprehend what is happening to the body. Dissociative Identity Disorder does exist, but with very specific criteria defined in the DSM-IV. "DID is characterized by two or more separate personalities with distinct postures, gestures, and ways of thinking. The person literally dissociates himself from a situation or experience that is too violent, traumatic, or painful to assimilate with his conscious self."[11] Understanding the development of multiple personalities is difficult, even for highly trained experts. "It is the most severe and chronic manifestation of the dissociative disorders that cause multiple personalities as defined in the DSM-IV, the main

---

[11] Web M.D. on *Dissociative Identity Disorder*. http://www.wedmd.com. Accessed 5/11/20.

psychiatry manual used to classify mental illnesses, and includes dissociative amnesia, dissociative fugue, and depersonalization disorder."[12] However, there is help out there for people with this troubling, complicated disorder.

The traumatized person must be given kind, compassionate, professional care. DID is a controversial, complicated, and convoluted disorder. It takes a great deal of time and commitment to treatment on the part of both therapist and survivor. The time involved depends on the individual being treated, the level of trauma experienced, and the amount of commitment to get well on the part of the survivor. It takes a great commitment and an investment of time that many therapists simply do not have for one reason or another. The survivor should ask questions and ensure that the therapist is someone with whom they will be able to interact and receive the necessary help and time. The therapist should be empathetic to trauma in the human experience. I believe that as Christians, we should not discount the help of psychological counselors. There are many that bring their expertise to bear and have much compassion toward people of all religions. The therapist must be chosen carefully. The therapist must understand these disorders and be experienced in helping with them.

There are several protective devices that a severely traumatized individual will employ for personal coping. Dissociative amnesia refers to the inability to recall important events of one's life and cannot be attributed to mere forgetfulness, which occurs during dissociation. When the person "becomes" another in order to cope with the devastation being experienced, he or she cannot remember any of the other personalities and their beliefs. The person "switches parts" so as not to remember; the phenomenon causes the person to feel safer inside, as it never feels safe to speak one's true name after certain types of traumas where the person was threatened with death. When the person begins to heal, co-consciousness occurs. The different "parts" become aware of the others and inner communication begins to happen.

---

[12] Ibid.

When a person with DID "switches parts," they become someone else, another personality, in order to deal with a particular pain or traumatic event. It is always easier if "someone else" takes the pain. Then the person does not have to feel the pain. This is a completely unconscious process. They will soon "switch" again, often into the previous "part," the different personality they were before, or perhaps even "someone different" still. This is dissociation, which refers to the ability of certain persons to "split" into different "parts" as a coping mechanism during an event that the person is unable to handle. The "part" the person lives in changes at different points in life. One can stay in a certain "part," or "alter" for years at a time, then seemingly for no reason, "switch" into a completely different "part" or "alter." Each "alter" or "part" has a different and necessary role in helping the whole person cope with life. I use "part" and "alter" interchangeably throughout this book.

Dissociative fugue is another protective device unconsciously used by a person with DID. When the trauma is too great, the person goes blank in their mind and just walks away from the trauma without remembering that trauma. The person will often return to their home or a safe place without remembering how they got there. It is even said that a person will return to their childhood home and be unable to remember traveling there. Persons with these disorders may also travel to another state or part of the world, then "switch parts" and be unable to remember the trip. Perhaps not only a temporary trip, as some persons are known to begin a completely different life. Rare, but true.

Dissociative fugue is the "sudden, unexpected travel away from home or one's customary place of work, with inability to recall one's past; confusion about personal identity, or the assumption of a new identity; or significant distress or impairment."[13] This troubling aspect of trauma survival is certainly possible, though somewhat unusual. According to the *Merck Manual*, a fugue state can be seen

---

[13] DSM-IV. *Dissociative Fugue*. http://www.cme.psychiatryonline.org. Accessed 5/12/20.

as an escape from responsibility, and cases take up only a fraction of a percentage of the population. "When in a fugue, people disappear from their usual routine and may assume a new identity, forgetting all or some of their usual life . . . [fugue] may develop as an alternative to suicidal or homicidal impulses . . . a fugue may last from hours to weeks, months, or occasionally even longer."[14] These are extreme circumstances, of course, but possible with severe trauma and could possibly account for some of the anonymity of some people living on the streets. It is not just escape from responsibility, it is a self-protective device.

Depersonalization disorder occurs as an aspect of DID, when a traumatized person has the sensation that they are not real, that they are a robot, plastic, or feel as if always in a dream. Catastrophizing is also common and one cannot get past thinking that they are in grave danger even while in quite safe conditions.[15] Life can be going just fine and the person may panic or look for danger. Hypervigilance is an aspect of catastrophizing and is listed in the symptoms above. The person feels safe while in direct danger because it feels normal to them; they sense normality in their bodies. They flashback to the past when danger felt normal and may have difficulty recognizing that they are now safe, even if they are in safe surroundings with safe people and are truly safe. It can take years to convince oneself that safety has arrived and that a healing pilgrimage is in progress. Danger feels safe and safety feels dangerous.

Under the umbrella of depersonalization is derealization. Derealization means that the person disconnects from their humanness and *senses* that one is not real, which is differentiated from *feeling* that one is unreal, suggesting an emotional reaction.[16] While some persons can experience this fleetingly, those who have the feelings constantly or have frequent recurrences are diagnosed

---

[14] The Merck Manuals Online Medical Library on *Dissociative Fugue*. http://www.merck.com. Accessed 5/1/20.

[15] Merck Manual Online. *Depersonalization/Derealization Disorder* http://www.merckmanuals.com.. Accessed 5/13/20.

[16] Ibid.

with depersonalization disorder. It can involve the sensation that the limbs are detached from the body.

Globalization, also under the umbrella of depersonalization disorder, involves "all or none," or "black and white" thinking. Those persons who have PTSD, DID, and or a panic disorder are likely to experience these troubling disorders. These disorders, as well as panic, are brought on by stress and trauma and not by drugs, alcohol, or other outside means.[17] I experienced all three: dissociative amnesia, dissociative fugue states, and depersonalization disorder. At this writing, I have been diagnosed with Dissociative Identity Disorder for 27 years; I am now healed but it was a process. I will tell of my healing in this work. Memories come in different forms; mental and physical or body memories being two.

"Body memories" are memories of sensory quality, not just the feeling of emotion. The body carries the senses; the senses reside in the body. The cognition must marry the body, meaning that one has to repeat the facts of the current reality over and over; the cognition and body must converge. The mind must be clear on reality and relieve the body of its distortions. These distortions have been present for a very long time, so persons must be encouraged to have patience with themselves in this process. Body memories are characterized by pain and various other sensations in the body with no apparent cause and are not attributed to simple stress. "Repressed memories are stored in the body. They may show up as unexplained symptoms where treatment after treatment does not work."[18] Mysterious illnesses occur when memories are deeply repressed in the human body and psyche.

Memories cause other phenomena as well. Similar to the flashbacks of PTSD are abreactions, which occur in DID. Abreactions are different in that the experience is relived rather than just seen as a flash. With abreactions come the sights, sounds, feelings, sensations,

---

[17] Ibid.

[18] Chrystine Oksana, *Safe Passage to Healing, A Guide for Survivors of Ritual Abuse* (New York: Harper Perennial, 1994), 126.

even tastes of the traumatic event. These occur with survivors of war, as do flashbacks.

The best plan of care for dissociative identity disorder and PTSD for the Christian is the pastoral counseling of discipleship in conjunction with psychological counseling. I say psychological counseling because of the expertise of many in the field who deal with DID, PTSD, Depression and such. Churches are becoming more aware and better able to handle these difficult diagnoses, but we are not completely there yet. People must be discipled in order to learn Scripture that has been twisted and perverted at times by abusers or misunderstood by the individual. The judgment of saying to an individual with these disorders, "if only you had more faith you would get over this" is repulsive. Pastoral counselors must be patient and give their time and attention without expecting too much too soon. It takes years to overcome these disorders.

Major Depression is also called Major Depressive Disorder. "Traumatic events during childhood, such as abuse or loss of a parent [of which I had both], may cause permanent changes in the brain that make you more susceptible to depression. Depression is a medical illness that involves the mind and body."[19] It can involve the whole person in every way. "Also called major depression, major depressive disorder and clinical depression, it affects how you feel, think, and behave. Depression can lead to a variety of emotional and physical problems." [20] It is a fitting companion to PTSD and DID, unfortunately. "More than just a bout of the blues, depression isn't a weakness, nor is it something that you can simply 'snap out' of. Depression is a chronic illness that usually requires long-term treatment, like diabetes or high blood pressure."[21] Taking medication for depression should therefore not be seen as taboo, but merely as correcting a physical disease. It is physical as it affects the chemical balance of the body in the brain.

---

[19] Mayo Clinic. *Major Depressive Disorder.* www.mayoclinic.com. Accessed 3/15/20.
[20] Ibid.
[21] Ibid.

I was diagnosed with Bipolar Disorder in 2013 by my primary care physician. I was angry to say the least when I was not told but found out six years later when going through my medical records. At that point, I had trouble coping with the diagnosis but have now come to terms with it. I think back on my early adult life and understand that I had the disorder. People live for years like I did without being diagnosed or treated and some never get diagnosed or treated in this life. "Bipolar Disorder is defined as a serious mental illness that causes unusual shifts in mood, ranging from extreme highs (mania) to low lows (depression) . . . it is difficult to carry out day-to-day tasks, go to work or school, and maintain relationships."[22] Bipolar I Disorder is characterized by extreme highs and extreme lows in mood and behavior. Bipolar II Disorder is characterized by less extreme highs called hypomanic states, yet depressive episodes are as severe as in Major Depressive Disorder or Bipolar I Disorder.[23] I have Bipolar II Disorder and have never had extreme manic episodes, just hypomania at intervals, and crippling depression at times.

In this work, I have been graphic at times about the details that caused me to "go to pieces" and, in other parts, not so graphic. I was only as graphic as I believed necessary to make my point on each issue. I sought to tell my story as completely as necessary to my task, and as it occurred in my healing journey. The issues I raise are presented more as they came up in my remembrance as I began to heal rather than chronological in my life. In this chapter is a concise explanation of these troubling chronic disorders and their symptoms, which I have experienced. My focus in this book is my story, my testimony, and information related to the disorders that have affected me, so as to attempt to provide assistance to others similarly affected or for those who care for those similarly affected.

I now know and have full conviction that it is not a requirement of healing to know every detail of every memory of every abusive

---

[22] Substance Abuse and Mental Health Services Administration. www.SAMHSA.gov. Accessed 3/17/2024.

[23] Ibid.

moment in life; I do not even think it possible. The same holds true that we do not remember every detail of every good and happy moment in life. Knowing for the sake of knowing is not important to memory recall, but knowing for the sake of learning how to correct any distortion in us and how it hinders our lives today is important.

PTSD is characterized by overwhelming stress, panic, and flashbacks. DID is characterized by dissociative amnesia, dissociative fugue, depersonalization (including globalization, catastrophizing, hypervigilance, and derealization), abreactions, body memories, identity confusion, and identity distortion. Bipolar Disorder has episodes of mania or hypomania (lesser manic states) and depressive episodes. Medication is needed to cope with the chemical process imbalance in the brain as far as medical science knows now.

Pastoral counseling is needed for the person with these disorders. The individual must experience compassion and care from the counselor and not judgment. It is wrong for a pastoral counselor to tell someone who has been chronically and traumatically abused and wounded to "just get over it" or "if you had enough faith reading this Scripture would be enough to get you over it." I have experienced both the good and the bad in this regard. Care and compassion are requirements to healing from these convoluted disorders.

Alters may be male and female in a female person or male and female in a male person. This does not indicate sexual preference in the individual, it is a matter of function. Male parts may give strength and feminine parts may give compassion and gentleness. This is not always the case, but both genders are common in persons with DID. There may be sexual identity issues in individuals with DID, but just having opposite alters does not define this. Persons left untreated will find that life does not work for them. Out of control living is usually the defining theme.

Alters are stuck at the age of their trauma and must "grow up" with the help of the Holy Spirit. If the abuse happened at age six causing an alter to form, that alter is still age six. However, the Holy Spirit can help and the work toward integration begins with surrender to the Holy Spirit of God. Only He can do the necessary work with the cooperation of the individual.

The person must also have co-consciousness where there is enough cooperation inside the person's soul to have full knowledge of all the parts. Integration is possible when all parts are "speaking" to each other and communicating "inside." Agreement in the system of a person's alters is required. I accomplished this by journaling conversations and imagery within my mind; this is not spiritualism to use imagery, it is utilizing the creative mind that God gave me. "We have the mind of Christ" (I Cor 2:16 NIV).

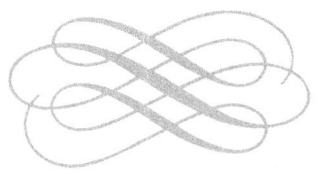

CHAPTER 1

TESTIMONY TO THE LIGHT

Then Jesus spoke to them . . . saying, "I am the
light of the world. He who follows Me shall not
walk in darkness but have the light of life."
(John 8:12).

In Him was life, and the life was the light of men.
(John 1:4).

I seek to give an orderly account of the faithfulness of my God. God has "a book of remembrance" (Malachi 3:16) and it is my desire to write an account of remembrance to God telling others of His awesome faithfulness. My goal in this work is to bring glory to God who has healed me. I am a redeemed child of God and have a redemptive story. God is my perfect Father. I seek to bring glory with my whole life to the One who has saved, healed, and delivered me.

I believe that Christ's desire is to heal people from the inner pain they have experienced on earth. He provides eternal life to anyone who is willing. He desires that all people receive eternal life with Him, but sadly not all receive Him. "But as many as received Him, to them He gave the right to become children of God, to those who believe in His name" (John 1:12). Many faith groups bring some peace to people of the world, but the Bible tells us that Jesus is the Prince of Peace (Isaiah 9:6).

The task I have is to give an account of my testimony, of how I was helped. In therapy, I had freedom to choose my own spiritual belief no matter what that might have been, even one that is far from Christianity. I will share my personal convictions in relation to my healing. I need to make this clear before continuing. Christ is the only way; I cannot say otherwise.

The Bible tells us that the human heart is wicked. "The heart is deceitful above all things, and desperately wicked; who can know it? I the Lord, search the heart" (Jeremiah 17:9, 10). God sees the truth of what is in the human heart even though the person may appear to others to be a righteous person with true motives toward God. "But the Lord said to Samuel, 'Do not look at his appearance or at his physical stature, because I have refused him [to be king of God's people in his day]. For the Lord does not see as man sees; for man looks at the outward appearance, but the Lord looks at the heart" (1 Samuel 16:7). The human heart is capable of utter degradation and the destruction of others.

The enemy of God and all who belong to God, the devil, wants to kill us and take away every trace of trust in Jesus in our hearts. He works overtime. He is a real enemy as the Bible teaches; we should be aware of his tactics. Now I see it as the opposition that comes to "all who desire to live godly in Christ Jesus" (2 Timothy 3:12). The Bible tells us that Satan is a created being; there is no dualism in the universe. God created Satan as an anointed cherub. Verses in the Book of Ezekiel tell us that he was beautiful and blessed in the beginning (Ezekiel 28:12-15). While the verses refer to the King of Tyre, they are understood by theologians as directly in relation to Satan. He was in heaven at the throne of God, yet pride destroyed him, and he fell (Isa 14:12-15). We are told that he "shall be brought . . . to the lowest depths of the pit" (Isaiah 14:15). He is a defeated foe, yet causes problems for us in our walk with God.

No human person is more powerful than the enemy of our souls, so humans should not be foolish in challenging him. God is, however, the enemy's Creator and defeated him long ago at Calvary. Jesus bruised his head (Genesis 3:15), the head of his power, when He died on the cross and rose again. God is all powerful and all knowing. There is no dualism in the universe. God has no rival. God is completely sovereign, omnipotent, omniscient, and omnipresent. We should neither pay too much attention to Satan nor be fascinated by him, yet neither should we ignore his existence. He was full of pride, but the Bible says that "God resists the proud, but gives grace to the humble. Therefore, submit to God. Resist the devil and he will flee from you. Draw near to God and He will draw near to you" (James 4:6-8). We worship God alone and look to Him for all the help we need to live and live well. I was never told these biblical truths, so I pass them on.

I believe it a necessary personal task to bring my story, show it for what it is, expose the darkness, and then show my pilgrimage to the Light of God. When I write of "we" or "us," I refer to the whole of humanity, with me as merely one individual of the whole or, at times, of the whole of the church of Jesus Christ, with me, again, as one individual within the whole. I will write things that are difficult for me to write, but in so doing I strive to bring hope to others who are hurt and wounded by life. The church must become a healing house for wounded sinners, a place for people to gather in supported fellowship. This is my desperate desire and prayer that people may go to church for healing.

The Golden Age of man in the nineteenth century left the world thinking perhaps man is truly good, has good deep in the heart and soul, and that man is progressing in goodness. This has been the topic of much ethical literature and debate. Philosophers were convinced that man is truly good in heart and soul, even without God. The twentieth century proved a different case, the case of man becoming more depraved instead of the previous optimistic opinion. Proof came through World Wars I and II, mass destruction of humans by humans in wars that left the world devastated. Further proof came with the cruelty of Adolph Hitler and Nazi Germany in their evil purpose of ethnic cleansing. Six million Jewish persons were tortured and killed as well as persons of various other ethnicities that did not meet their cruel specifications of genetics. These people were cruelly tortured, maimed, and destroyed in unthinkable horrors in the cause of one race believing themselves superior to all others, utter blackness of the human heart. Well, this black heartedness lives on in some persons: those without God. Without God man is depraved.

Christ loves His church and in spite of all that people do wrong, the church is still God's choice for advancing His kingdom on earth. As true Christians, we serve a Triune God, the 3 in 1. I refer to three *persons* and not three aspects of God, not three changeable modes, but distinct persons. The first person of the Trinity is the Father, the second person is the Son, Jesus Christ, and the third person is the Holy Spirit. The Holy Spirit is a person and not an "it" as is sometimes said. It is appalling to me to hear people say that God is a "multiple personality." God never changes and has no pathology in Him. He is forever unchangeable and perfect in every way.

The Bible teaches the 3 in 1 concept of the Trinity so that we could understand better; most of us understand relationship better than some other heavier theological concepts, though we can never understand God fully. The Father sent His Son Jesus, who came willingly to die in our place on the cross so that we can have a relationship with a holy God. God made a way for us to be with Him for eternity through the cross, "for the message of the cross is foolishness to those who are perishing, but to us who are being saved, it is the power of God" (1 Corinthians 1:18). The Holy Spirit is the Spirit of Jesus Christ and all three are one, the one God Whom we serve as Christians.

Jesus was crucified, died, was buried, appeared on earth, then rose to heaven. God said to His Son Jesus, "Sit at My right hand till I make Your enemies Your footstool" (Hebrews 1:13). He is fully Man and was therefore able to die as the substitute for all our sins, having identified with us. "For we do not have a High Priest who cannot sympathize with our weaknesses, but was in all points tempted as we are, yet without sin" (Hebrews 4:15). He is fully God, "therefore He is also able to save to the uttermost those who come to God through Him, since He always lives to make intercession for them" (Hebrews 7:25). Jesus left the church in the hands of His disciples, who became the Holy Spirit-filled apostles following Pentecost (Acts 2:1-4). As true believers, we are all in the process of sanctification, so that we may "be preserved blameless at the coming of our Lord Jesus Christ (1 Thessalonians 5:23). In the meantime, we are imperfect.

The true church consists of imperfect people who fall on the mercy of God for salvation and eternal life. All human institutions are run by humans and are therefore flawed. Make no mistake about it, I love God and wish to see justice and healing for wounded people. After I became a Christian, I was able to remember what happened to me as a child, and God and I began the long process of healing and understanding of His love for all people. My only goal is to seek glory for His name and His name alone.

I believe God's grace has propelled me to His Light and it is my desire to share my pilgrimage in the hope that others may find this illumination. I write of my faith in God, of my childhood pain, and of information to assist others in the pilgrimage of their own lives. Please seek out well-balanced professional counselors, psychologists, and psychiatrists who specialize in treating traumatic abuse survivors. The therapist should be one who has empathy for the experience of the trauma survivor and is willing to invest time in treating them.

My hope is also to provide information to care providers of all disciplines including clergy who seek to help persons affected by these all-encompassing life issues. I have written from the perspective of a human being who is in touch with the human experience of traumatic abuse. I thrive today due to help given to me, much determination on my part and, first and foremost, God's grace.

From earliest childhood, I remember having one goal in mind for my life: to achieve "normal." However, there was no recognition of the unanswered questions lurking in the back of my mind, such as, what is normal? Is anyone normal? How will I know once I've arrived at "normal? Or is normal even possible? It seems the difficulty is in the terminology. I really wanted to be happy and free from fear, but did not know how to express it at the time. I wanted what other people seemed to have, which was happiness, confidence, and freedom to speak their mind. I also wanted to be free of night terrors, which were very common in my young life. I was confused by the terminology and meaning of the elusive word "normal." Could "normal" be a synonym for "successful?" I wondered. From my teen years on, to the distant onlooker, my life was successful. At closer glance, however, there were only certain aspects that were successful.

Friendship was success; I had good friends in church and to me this was good success. After two years of working full-time in offices post-high school, then nursing school, nursing school graduation, raising two sons to the best of my ability and being known as an honest and trustworthy woman, mother, and nurse was "success." What I had no knowledge of was that my life matters, simply because I exist. Every person has intrinsic worth and value. My life has intrinsic value because I am alive and have a Creator (Genesis 1:1; John 1:1-3) and Savior (Matthew 27; 28:1-20) who thought me worthy of relationship as He does every other person on earth.

Being a follower of Christ is not about being in a frou-frou, soft, warm and fuzzy religion with a weak or sissy god; neither is it being tied to a harsh, hard, uncaring God who created the world then turned His time and attention away from us out of boredom and lack of love. It is about finding true love and true purpose in life. The true and mighty God is love and it is my desire to convey this truth.

A word about deliverance concerning these disorders of DID and PTSD; I believe in deliverance from demonic entities because it is biblical. I have received deliverance from demonic entities, but alters are not demons. In this I waiver from some counselors. It wounds alters to try to cast them out of a person when alters are wounded children who just need healing and understanding. There may be demons hiding behind alters and influencing alters I understand; these must be dealt with of course. In the beginning of my Christian pilgrimage when I was first saved, I was bound in rage and bitterness in regard to men, church men, family men, those who had hurt me, abused me, and tormented my life. I received deliverance and it changed my whole countenance and attitude. I was prayed over with deliverance prayers for peace after the initial deliverance and received a great deal of peace. In conjunction with counseling, I believe deliverance to be useful as long as the alters are treated with care.

I do not doubt that God can do anything He so desires because He is God, Creator of all, but He did not choose to heal me all at once from DID. I had to talk about it, talk about it, and talk about it more for seven years before I came to some resolution. I had to relive, re-experience repeatedly, pray about it, and believe that I was making progress in God. I believe He has us work out our deliverance and healing. I also do not believe that "parts" are demons as I have stated before in this work. Self-love is necessary for healing. Self-loathing is common in DID and must be dealt with in therapy and /or pastoral counseling. I thought I was poison inside. The person with DID must become a parent for their parts and love and care for them. I know what it feels like to have DID and be misunderstood and misunderstand myself.

Individuals with DID must have patience with the less desirable or seemingly evil parts who are usually the most wounded parts of themselves. The parts do not go away, they are incorporated into the original personality after they are healed, and this includes salvation of each part. Each must decide for himself or herself about salvation with assistance from the host individual. This is a disorder that demands much cooperation inside the individual. There must be cooperation and unity among alters with following the Lord. In a Christian all parts must agree or the person is double-minded and "a double-minded man is unstable in all his ways" (James 1:8). I use her and him interchangeably denoting mankind as a whole.

Prayer is necessary for healing because the presence of God must be brought into each situation; however, we must never make the mistake of revealing individuals' traumas for the purpose of helping someone "know how to pray" for that person. God knows the situation and people do not need to know details in order to pray for a hurting person. This was done to me, which was very hurtful because the people who were told about me in turn told the leader of a Christian mission I was working with a few months later all about what I had experienced in my childhood. This information led to my dismissal from the work at the mission. The leader told me she was afraid of what I might do because I must be abnormal. I was devastated. I was also told I did not have enough faith to be in ministry because I was on medication for depression. Depression is a chemical disease that requires medication sometimes just like high blood pressure or diabetes. We can be overmedicated as a rule in this society, but there are times when some medication is essential to living with depression and other disorders.

I have had a lot of hurts in church in my pilgrimage from people who did not know how to help me or did not care to help me. Many pastors/ministers believe people should just come to church faithfully, give their money, and not bother the minister. Some churches are focused on evangelism only and believe this is the only ministry of the church. I beg to differ. Healing people is very important for the edification of the church to prepare members to minister in Christ's name. I have been kicked out of church, fired from a volunteer ministry position and gossiped about. A pastor kissed me in the sanctuary when I met with him to learn about theology and seminary. I did not want anything like this to happen. He told his wife that I did this to him. He told his congregation as well. I left that church in shame though I had done nothing wrong. I have been yelled at, cursed at, controlled and manipulated by a cult church situation, gossiped about some more, and told that the childhood abuse was my fault and that I was responsible for it. These were very deep wounds that took years to overcome.

God is bigger than all that however, and I am healed. I am thankful for all the godly ministry I have received in my healing journey, significant in spite of the hurts. Many wonderful ministers have come alongside me; many of these have been seminary professors where I attended. I have been healed by their kindnesses. It "takes a village to raise a child" (African proverb) or a dissociative person. It takes a communal effort of many people raising children and dissociative people in harmony. Many wonderful representatives of the true God have come into my life for which I am very thankful.

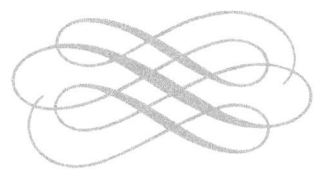

CHAPTER 2

DARKNESS WILL NOT WIN

*These things I have spoken to you, that in Me you may
have peace. In the world you will have tribulation, but
be of good cheer, I have overcome the world.*
(John 16:33).

*And the Lord will deliver me from every evil work
and preserve me for His heavenly kingdom. To
Him be glory forever and ever. Amen!*
(2 Timothy 4:18).

PTSD does not cripple me. DID does not define me. It is not who I am, nor who I was. I am not "a DID," "a crazy," or "needy," implying that I am unable to believe and function as other persons. I am simply someone who has a healing story to tell in the attempt to help others along their own personal healing path. I am someone who God graced to become well and whole and to pass this message on to others along the way with my testimony. I am a healer.

Henri J.M. Nouwen in his book, *The Wounded Healer* describes a person who has a passion for healing. Therein he refers to persons who have been severely wounded who find a measure of healing and then desire to bring healing and restoration to others through

Christ. Healing is what I care about, what I strive for, to help, to heal, to restore, to make right any way that I possibly can.

I have been in the helping field as a registered nurse since I was twenty years old; I care about healing. I plan to be a healer for the remainder of my days; it is my destiny, part of God's plan for my life. My healing journey goes on and this pilgrimage carries new meaning, a new life of its own. I am convinced that it is necessary for me to tell my story. Though troubled once, my life has purpose, and the main goal of this life for me is to aid others in their healing path through knowing God's love for them. There is hope in life for severely traumatized individuals.

I grew up in a middle-class American family in the suburbs of a large city and had friends in school. My friends and I played games such as a Ouija board and had séances, not very sophisticated séances; we played really. I had slumber parties, as did my friends, where we played the games. My family saw nothing wrong with these games. I went to church with my friends and sang in the youth choir. My family seemed very "normal" and typical from the outside. My family always appeared to be the all-American family, though there were deep dark underlying secrets that even I was not aware of at the time. I had no knowledge of a good, loving, benevolent God; only one who was harsh, hard, and critical of His creation. The 1960s was a turbulent era in religion in America. The New Age Movement was becoming strong in the 1960s. A rare family held to the traditional beliefs of Christianity amid the dawning of the Age of Aquarius.

My dad had been raised in an extremely poor family on a farm in Colorado and traveled a few states away to make a life for himself after his college days. He was educated and succeeded in making a comfortable life for himself and his family. He saw himself as a self-made man; he was proud. We were by no means wealthy when I was growing up, but we had enough. We had money for food to eat and a good home to live in. My parents taught us to work and make our own way. My parents were educated in college. I love my family very much and at the time thought we were the perfect family. Daddy was a World War II veteran who had served in Europe during the war as an accountant with the assignment of counting war casualties. He had an accounting degree from the University of Texas at Austin, so this is why he had the war assignment. I am glad that he had that opportunity to serve his country. He was very proud of America and was an avid patriot.

I have full consciousness of some of these terrors. My grandfather was my dad's dad and was abusive to my dad when he was growing up, I am told. He was also abusive to my brother, he told me, and he was to me also. I do not know if he was abusive to my older sisters or not. They are much older than me and we have not talked about it. My grandfather was a 33rd degree Freemason as was my dad. My uncle was also. My grandfather was very serious about Freemasonry and was called "anointed high priest" according to his Masonic Bible inscription. I was about four to six years old when abuse happened to me. It was systematic ritual abuse in a closed children's home with trafficked children, in another state from where I lived. They told many lies and manipulated and controlled the children there. They performed many "bad tricks" to make us believe we were evil and had done bad things, even murder. I do not remember my exact age, but it was likely between four and eight. He lived in Kansas, and we visited him there. He also visited our house when my sisters got married. My grandfather died when I was 10 years old, the same year my mother's mother died. His abuse was sexual and spiritual; I was afraid of him. I became a Rainbow Girl when I was 12-15, this is the girls' group of Freemasonry. At the time, I did not have clear memories of what had happened to me. I have since renounced my involvement with Freemasonry.

God had His hand on me all my life. He encouraged me at points along the way, even at a very young age. When I got scared or hurt, I always sang Jesus Loves Me in my heart, sometimes aloud. I believed the words to the song "Jesus Loves Me." No one could take away my belief or my song, the song of my heart. I learned this particular song at either a Sunday school or a Vacation Bible School. I believed that I could therefore find God in the Bible, which is the Word of God. This is what the song came to symbolize to me.

Jesus Loves Me

Jesus loves me this I know
For the Bible tells me so,
Little ones to Him belong,
They are weak but He is strong.
Yes, Jesus loves me,
Yes, Jesus loves me,
Yes, Jesus loves me,
The Bible tells me so.[24]

I knew at that age that Jesus loved me because of this redemptive song. I believed deep in my heart that "Jesus Loves Me." though I was told forcefully, "Jesus does not love you. God hates you and you are bound to go to hell!" Prior to learning this song, I believed what the abusers said. I believed I was evil, or poison to others. I was often told these wicked words, which caused confusion in my young mind. I remember believing that I killed someone, devastating to my young life. It really damaged me. I became dissociative through these events. But Jesus kept me and drew me to himself. I continued to believe in him and in the song. Another event that happened to cause dissociation was getting lost in a military hospital, which I call an accidental trauma.

I was with my dad when I was three or four. He worked at a profession that worked closely with the military. He visited the military hospital in the city where we lived and took me with him that day. I do not remember what the incident was, of course, at age four and did not remember this for some years. I dreamed it all my life though. I finally started dealing with it when I was in counseling; the nightmare went away when I brought it into full consciousness. We were in the emergency room when helicopters began to bring in men on stretchers. These men had been burned and were calling out for the doctors and nurses to let them die.

---

[24] Hymn by William B. Bradbury (1816-1868) and Anna B. Warner (1820-1915).

The burns were severe and some of the men did die. I saw stretchers with men covered over with sheets in a makeshift morgue. Of course, I did not know what these were at the time but know now in my adult understanding of what I saw. I got lost from Daddy and ended up on an elevator. It opened at what I can only imagine was the Burn Unit. There were men covered in bandages and moaning. I do not remember how I got back with my dad, but my subconscious mind never let me forget this severe incident. Severe because I was four years old, severe for any child. I also remember being in the autopsy room with my dad and the doctor.

I did not feel loved by my dad. He was impatient and short with me. He called me weak because I cried a lot. I took these things into myself because I was already wounded at a young age. I really thought I was weak and stupid. I believed many lies about myself and my self-esteem suffered. I loved my dad very much though. I felt very ambivalent about my family members. My dad worked very hard for his family. He was a businessman doing executive work. He was gone in the evening quite a bit. We only saw him for dinner, and he was off again. My mother was sick when I was a young child with severe cluster headaches, migraine-like headaches that caused misery and despair for her and this led to my being a nurse later in life as I helped my grandmother care for her. My family had enough resources to live comfortably. I never heard "I love you" from anyone in my family of origin my whole life until I was 40 and had attempted suicide. My parents said I was supposed to know that I was loved. It just was not said in my family. It was not only me. From my family, I learned well how to be obedient, to do exactly what I was told to do. My dad was a disciplinarian, as was my mother. The ambivalence was strong; I both loved and feared them.

Darkness tried to overtake me when I experienced a traumatic loss in my life when my beloved grandmother died when I was ten-years old. I cannot write of my life without telling of the trauma of this event. She was eighty-one years old when she passed away of a heart attack. She had been my primary caregiver since I was a two-year-old child and she came to live with our family. I could talk to her more than I could talk to any other person. With her, I felt loved. She never said, "I love you," but I felt loved. She comforted me and was the only one who did in my home. I could not tell her the "secrets" that lurked and, therefore, could receive no comfort directly for the traumas that were happening to me, but she allowed me to sleep in her bed and there I felt safe. She was nurturing and because of her, I believe I learned to be a nurturer. Mama gave me more nurture than any other person.

Mama was my mother's mother. Her nurturing was a tool of life for me. Through the good things I received from her, I was able to love my own children when they were born. She never laughed at me when I was terrified by what I saw, heard, and experienced at night. She comforted me after my night terrors, which helped me greatly. I loved her dearly and was devastated when she went to visit my aunt and passed away there. The pain and grief ran very deep. I remember having been angry with her before she left. After her death, the guilt was enormous. I had not really meant to be angry, but because I had thought it, I believed I caused her death. I know this is magical thinking of a child, but it was the young child in me that believed that way. I felt I had no one in the world who understood me. I was not close to my mother at all, or my dad at the time.

When Mama passed, I knew I had lost my true mother. It was a traumatic experience for me as a child, but now after healing from my pain, I can put it in perspective. Yes, it wounded me deeply, but I knew she never would have left me intentionally. I miss her terribly to this day, and sometimes still cry over her. One thing I never understood was that neither she nor anyone else could explain to me the night terrors, the visions, or the memories I had as a child. I would have thought that Mama would have tried to help me through the visions and terrors I had, unless most of them were real occurrences. I was a tormented child; tormented by nightmares, tormented in my mind. I believe Mama did not know how to help me or she would have.

My childhood pastor gave me strength after Mama's death with his words: "You will see her again." I held to his words for many years. It was God's way of telling me I would not be alone forever as I felt then. In all that God never left me, though I did not have revelation at that time of His presence with me. I had forgotten the sense of His presence I knew at age four.

After Mama's death, I was blessed to see my mother well and able to engage in life. She had been placed on medication for the terrible migraine headaches that she had been tormented with and was much better. This was the grace of God, though I did not realize it at the time. She was more motherly then. God loved me when I did not know His presence and power to live the Christian life. Life was good when I was in high school. It was not perfect at home; my parents were controlling and distant. But I had a great time in the band, drama club, and church activities. I had great friends, some of which I still have today. I had great friends in church. My mother was more involved than my dad with me and my activities and church.

Daddy was a leader in the church, a Sunday school teacher of the men. My family went to churches that did not give a clear presentation of the Gospel of Jesus Christ though. I did not really know what true Christianity looked like. Our church had a very loving pastor when I was a tween and early teen, but our pastor finished his career as a minister when I was about sixteen. I believe God had given me a chance as a teenager to live a life in Christ. I had an experience at a church camp at age fourteen that could have turned my life in that direction. I prayed and believed God was real. When I returned from church camp, my parents mocked my faith. I started on the right way toward God but was confused when my parents laughed at me. I began to believe it was too difficult to be a Christian. I lost trust in the church also.

The reason I lost trust was that my church was going through a major church split at the time. The pastor and associate pastor had some issues and there was some sexual misconduct happening. The church split and it seems my family was in the middle of the debate. A previous church that my family was involved with had a devastating split a few years earlier. Trust was waning in me. Church splits wound and devastate people and families, particularly if the people are not strong in the Lord. Splits can lead people to leave the church as did some members of my family. I was the youngest in my family and previous church hurts happened to my parents and siblings.

Growing up, I had some opportunities, such as school activities and music. My parents encouraged and focused on the importance of education and music. I learned to appreciate fine music by going to symphonies with my piano teacher and parents. I was given music lessons all through my growing-up years. I was a pianist and organist as a child and teen; I played for church groups and was a talented musician. Others planned for me to become a concert pianist, but it was not my dream. True, it had been my idea to begin piano lessons at the age of seven, but I just wanted to enjoy the instrument.

Music was escapism for me as a child, as I had many pleasurable hours of practice. I was an obedient student; no one had to ask me to practice, I simply lost myself in the music. I did not have to think about pain, hurt, and guilt when I practiced. I did not dream of ever being a famous musician. I simply wanted to enjoy the music and fought against the others' dreams of my being a concert pianist. I had wanted to play contemporary music and play by ear, but my classical training would not allow me to be free enough to learn. I loved the music but did not want a career in it.

I had participated in piano competitions as a young teen and had known the pressure of the performance track. I was ordered to perform memorized pieces without prior notice any time my parents had company at home. I was instructed to play outside our home, as well, for other events. I was a perfectionist, and this caused me much stress as I struggled to be in the proper sub state (the personality that knew how to play well). Switching parts was very stressful as I tried to look normal. As a teen, I took some drugs to try to relieve the pain I felt. When I came home and had to try to play for my parents, I could not remember the music; therefore, I was humiliated at times and my parents were upset with me. And I was not at all interested in that pressure or the pressure that I knew would come with being a concert pianist for the public. I wanted to live a life of service.

I went to work in an office straight out of high school, which was boring to me, but was a good interim job until I discovered what I wanted to do in life. After two years of office work, I followed my heart to nursing school, two years after high school, and worked with all my strength. I fulfilled my dream and worked very hard as a registered nurse. It was a good living to raise my family. I was a good citizen, a good American. I was living for the American dream, as a typical, young American was encouraged to do then. Nevertheless, I felt I was playing a very foul and fraudulent existence. I did not feel "real" or "normal," but fought these feelings of depersonalization fiercely. I knew deep in me that my heart oozed black poison and that if anyone got too close, I would ooze over into them, and they would die. I did not feel loved by God or people.

I had productive alters that accomplished some things like "success" in nursing school. I had a nurse alter that made decent grades in school and did my nursing job well. This alter was completely focused on being a nurse (it was part of me of course). I say completely because I could shut out everything else and just be a nurse at the time, which was good for my work ethic. The only problem was that when I was in therapy, I could not always function on a given day and I took many mental health days, though I never called it that. I just called in sick. When people started to get to know me too well, I changed jobs so that my work history showed way too many jobs. I could not stay at my job long. I could not face anyone knowing my diagnosis. I have come a long way. I no longer call in sick at my job. Now I figure I must try to help someone else by exposing my story. I cannot help but testify how God healed me. I no longer hide like I did for so long.

When I was working on my second nursing job, I had to go for a tuberculosis test (TB). The test was positive, and they did a chest x-ray on me. The physician told me that I had had TB as a child because I had the scars to prove it. I was put on prophylactic medications for one year to prevent a recurrence. How did I have tuberculosis as a child, and no one ever knew it? Hmm . . . After 25 years in Medical/Surgical nursing, I worked for five years as a hospital chaplain, then as an RN sonographer for 2-3 years, then as a behavioral health nurse.

I love the psychiatric patients. One of them said about me today, "she understands us." This was a great compliment from her. If she only knew how close I was to them. I am only well by God's great grace, but I am well and dedicated to helping and healing where I can. "But for the grace of God go I,"[25] I have heard it said.

In spite of these feelings of being poison, I struggled to live up to my parents' expectations of being an educated person and being successful in the world. I had a strong ambivalence in me to live up to these expectations as well as to live up to the life my husband wanted to live when I got married at age 19. My parents' way won out. My parents had taught me to strive for the American Dream, and that I did, beginning in my first marriage. I followed hard after this dream with education, career, making money, marriage, children, and a three-bedroom two-bath brick home in the suburbs. I was super-responsible and thought I was the ruler of my life for a few years. In my thirties, I began to unravel in my mind. I was not a stable person inside myself and while I worked hard on the outside (nursing work, raising children), on the inside I was mush and it showed at times. Other times I was able to hold it together. I did not realize my instability however and thought I had it all together.

I regret to this day that I was divorced twice, but nothing can change what happened. I did not know how to cope with life and marriage. My children had gone to live with their dad and grandparents at their request when they were tweens and it devastated me. They were pushed to this decision, so therefore, I do not hold it against the children. I so wish that I had known the power of the Gospel to change lives. My life was a train wreck, and all my good efforts were fruitless to control my own life. The rejection by my husbands and my parents as well as my children leaving my home was too much for me to bear, but this is what it took to bring me to my knees and cause me to give up the rights to my own life. I could not bear the pain alone.

In recent years, I have asked my children's forgiveness many times over for the hurt I caused them because I had not known what

---

[25] Quote from John Bradford (1510-1555), English Reformer and martyr for his faith.

else to do but divorce; they told me that they forgave me. It took me many years to forgive myself, but I finally did. It was critical to my healing. I told my children about the abuse from my childhood when I first found out, but do not talk about all that with them anymore. They treated me with kindness and love when I told them. I am so very thankful that my sons and I have relationships today. I believe that God restored our relationships and will further restore them.

So, a timeline for the events of a portion of my life are as follows; I believed in Jesus' love for me when I was four years old when I sang Jesus Loves Me. At age eleven, we went to church having a wonderful pastor. At age sixteen, my pastor retired. In his place was the minister that split our church with his sexual antics. At age seventeen, I met my first husband and married when I was nineteen. I still went to church because I was a church organist and was working in the church. But my life was far from God. I switched back and forth constantly. At 22, I became the mother of a wonderful boy Brandon. At 23, I became a registered nurse. At 24, I became the mother of a beautiful boy named Clint. I love these sons with all my heart. I now have six grandchildren who I love greatly. I have five granddaughters and one grandson. They are named in order of birth: Rainie, Kaycee, Ryhder, Caroline, Breanna, and Braelyn. I love these children so much and love to tell them about Jesus' love for them. I have two daughters-in-law who I love and am so proud of; Brandon's wife is Adrienne and Clint's wife is Mallory. I am so proud of all of these people in my life. I am a cookie-baking Grandma. The grandkids and I love to bake together. We also love holidays together and amusement parks.

TESTIMONY

I want to bring glory to God with my testimony. God is good; He has completely changed my life. He has called me to His service, and I am very thankful. I surrendered my life to Christ at age 36. I did not believe that God could love me. I was too full of sin. I was traumatized as a child. At age 4 or so, I remember believing in Jesus and singing "Jesus Loves Me." I believed in Jesus because of a Vacation Bible School I attended at a young age. I told my parents what I had learned about Jesus. They laughed and told me never to talk about Jesus again. I never knew why my parents were so against Jesus and His Gospel. Hurts that happened in church is what I understand now about them. After that I kept my mouth shut – for a few years.

At age 10, my dear grandmother who I called Mama passed away. She raised me up until this age. I was absolutely devastated and afraid of what would happen to me. I felt that at the time, in my household, she was the only one who cared for me. I felt alone in the world. Right before her death, I had begun going to church with friends from school. The pastor of the church comforted me with the words "you will see her again." However, the church did not give a clear presentation of the Gospel of Jesus Christ and was focused on preaching on social issues of the time. "The Gospel is the power of God unto salvation" (Rom 1:16). But I did not know the Gospel, I did not hear the Gospel, and I did not have salvation.

As a young teen of 14, I went to church camp. God was drawing me. I had a spiritual experience that caused me to believe that Jesus is real. I told my parents about it because I was excited. Again, they laughed and mocked and shut it down. I learned to keep my mouth shut about my faith. At age 17, I decided in my heart that it was too difficult to live the Christian life. I had been disillusioned by a terrible event in my church. I turned toward sin and away from God. I willingly sinned with my boyfriend who I later married. He was not a Christian. This led to many years of heartache, abuse, and emotional pain. Now I know that we all need a Savior, a daily walk with Christ. But it would be years before I learned it. I did not believe that God could love me. I was full of guilt, shame, and fear. I became an RN at age 23 hoping that I could be "good enough" for God to love. It was all about works as I did not know grace. I was married and had two beautiful sons who were my whole world. I was a church organist for 15 years as a teen and young adult, but my heart was far away from God.

I became burned-out in my career at age 31. I was severely depressed. I had panic attacks. I had married for a second time, but it did not work out. We were both emotional messes and were not Christians. I had panic attacks. I turned to alcohol and relationships with men to try to soothe my broken heart. But of course, I only got hurt more deeply. A life of sin leads to hurt and pain. I had not learned the Ten Commandments in church, but I broke the commandments anyway. This is the sin nature of man.

In September of 1995 I gave my life over to the Lord Jesus Christ and my life changed forever. I was in a desperate state. I felt like a complete failure in marriage, motherhood, and as a human being at this time. I felt utterly incompetent in every area of life. Guilt was eating me alive, gnawing away at me. Shame was constant; I felt like a total failure. I felt guilty and evil, so I called out to God to kill me. I could not stand life anymore, but I did not try to end it. I really thought He would kill me because I had turned away from Him. I deserved death and hell. Though I begged Him to kill me, He did not. Instead, He gave me new life!

As an adult, I had been miserable being a nurse after so many years. Burn-out had taken over; daily life as a nurse became harder to cope with and the work became more difficult to concentrate on as my life fell apart. I had tried working in every area of nursing that I could to see if maybe I was just displaced and needed to find my niche as a nurse, but no place fit me. I did not fit me. I believed that I had been helping people as a nurse, but who cared to help me? I needed help desperately. I had given and given and given. Nevertheless, on that September day, I was sick and tired of my seemingly insignificant life. I was sick with bronchial pneumonia in both lungs and had the addictions of alcohol, cigarettes, and relationships with men that I could not break on my own. But Jesus gave me a revelation from His Word on His love for me. "I have loved you with an everlasting love. Therefore, with lovingkindness I have drawn you" (Jer 31:3). Jesus continued to draw me to Himself.

I had a true touch from Jesus that day in 1995. I was never the same after that. After I surrendered my heart to Christ that day and believed His Word, I told my parents again. Again, they laughed and mocked, but I refuse to ever stop talking about Jesus now. They came to understand that my conversion was real. Daddy told me, "I knew you were called to the ministry!" He was not happy about it. Well, I will continue to tell my story, but this was the start of it. God gave me the Great Commission and told me to "Go ye" and to "Feed the hungry." I have tried to obey every way that I know how. The Great Commission is our task on this earth. I take my task very seriously and go to tell everyone I can about Jesus Christ and His Gospel.

❧❧❧

I want to share one word about nursing burn-out. So many people in the situation I was in feel trapped in their profession. I have known those who have died at a young age of heart attack and stroke, crushed under the heavy load placed on them. Some committed suicide. I have known of nurses who died in motor vehicle accidents falling asleep at the wheel because they were overworked and exhausted. We are not good at caring for ourselves. Many nurses are hurting and wounded people, crushed under life's burdens; only the Lord God can sustain life. I know there are healthcare workers everywhere in the same predicament; nursing is the only field I know of first-hand. Caring for family, friends and wounded people whose needs are unending wounds us. Trying to bind up the wounds of others wounds us terribly. It is ministry – hard ministry. We cannot do this work in our own strength; we need the strength of God.

When I began to try to return to God, the first Scripture I saw and began to memorize was Psalm 51, King David's Psalm of repentance. This Psalm has been the most important Scripture for me in turning back to God, for repentance from my rebellion and all my sin, and for forgiving myself.

> Wash me thoroughly from my iniquity and cleanse me from my sin. For I acknowledge my transgressions, and my sin is always before me. Against You, You only,

have I sinned, and done this evil in Your sight – that You may be found just when You speak, and blameless when You judge. Behold I was brought forth in iniquity and in sin my mother conceived me. Behold You desire truth in the inward parts and in the hidden part You will make me to know wisdom. . . Create in me a clean heart O God, and renew a steadfast spirit within me (Psalm 51: 2-6, 10).

This pivotal Scripture in my life carried new meaning, even beyond my repentance and turning back to God. Verse 6 speaks of "truth in the inward parts and in the hidden part You will make me know wisdom." I held to this verse in my path through DID, believing that God meant what He said. I knew I was at the Lord's mercy. It was a great step of faith for me after I had been taught that God did not care. I knew the Judge of all the earth was who I was trusting, and it terrified me, to say I had the fear of God was an understatement. I prayed and cried the whole Psalm. I did not know if God was truly loving, but I really hoped that the Bible was true. I later found out that it is true, fully true.

I listened to teaching tapes by selected Bible teachers and followed along in my Bible for about ten hours a day for a month. One day, suddenly, God opened my eyes, and I received a revelation of God's love for me, a Father's love. I also saw for the first time the Great Commission in Matthew 28:18-20. Yes, I say suddenly because I do not know how it happened, only that the world was very different all of a sudden. I had renewed hope of salvation, as the preachers were saying, and a renewed sense of purpose for my life, what I craved. At that pivotal moment that the Lord showed me the Great Commission, I had been praying, "God, please let me do something else besides be a nurse, change me, change my life – or let me die – please!" I fully believed He was able to kill me at any time. I cried out to God, saying, "Oh God, let me die! I hate it here! Take me away to a good place!" I displayed some faith in His benevolence to take me to a good place, even in my cries. I prayed this over and over, and again. I had prayed this in my car, just screaming it at the top of my lungs where no one else could hear.

Oh, how I begged to die! Nevertheless, He just loved me and I sensed Him saying, "No, child; you are here and it is not time to go now." I had developed a case in my burned-out life of discontent, which did not surprise God. He was changing me from the inside out, changing the entire focus of my life. I would soon see people's lives changed, not by saving their lives temporally with medicines, surgery, and other medical treatments, but by heart surgery from the heavenly heart Surgeon, the Ultimate Lifesaver Jesus Christ, the One who can save lives. Yes, I gave up the rights to my life. I came to the end of myself.

I had a sense of the Lord's call at this point and His gentle whisper deep within my spirit, saying, "You can work for Me." His work was my new purpose in life. I burst out of my room in my parents' home, shouting, "God is real! I believe in Him! You can know Him for yourself! Satan is real and he wants to kill us!" It is truly a miracle that my parents did not have me committed somewhere in a mental ward. They thought I had completely "lost it." However, they could not deny the results of my conversion to Christ, most of which they could see. They knew I was gravely ill with pneumonia on Saturday. I woke up the next morning, a Sunday morning, completely well, with no trace of infection in my lungs and all addictions had ceased instantly.

I went to church that morning at a new church in a nearby city, beginning a new life. I had immediately stopped smoking that Saturday, the day of my conversion. I never picked up a cigarette again, though I had struggled hard for three years to quit that awful habit prior to this incident. My parents did not know about the alcohol or the men to my knowledge, but those cravings were broken and were never a problem again in the same way. God gave me a radical salvation and deliverance; I was greatly encouraged in my life. When I found Him, or rather, when He found me, I began to desire to live again and, for the first time, to truly live.

My family did not agree with my decision to enter the Bible

College that I did when I was 36. My parents did not believe in the supernatural aspect of God and said that if I went there, I would lose my mind because it was a charismatic Bible College. They laughed at my newfound faith. I knew that I was called to go there; I was determined to obey the Lord and His calling. I was greatly troubled, to say the least. I was troubled by the turmoil in the church, troubled by my family fighting against my faith, and troubled by the hidden terrors that lingered in my soul just below my consciousness. They really laughed when I played the tambourine for them but I did not care.

My desire had been to go to Bible College, so I could get to know the Bible. I found out about the college at the church I attended right after my conversion. I applied right away and three months later, I was in college. I had hit bottom and was saving my life by going to Bible College. It gave my life new meaning and purpose. It was one of the happiest moments of my life. However, I did not know even the most basic children's Bible stories. I bought a book of Bible stories, the kind that children learn from; I began to learn. God is faithful and brought me so far because I was so eager to learn, a grace from Him, I believe. I have studied ever since and am a lifelong learner. I entered seminary a few years later, a seemingly impossible task. I never thought I was intelligent enough to go to seminary. I had such low self-esteem and had been told for so long that I was ignorant and inadequate. Therefore, these years have brought healing and deliverance of my deep shame, guilt, and the pain of my life.

My mother has seen continued spiritual growth in me ever since and has come to accept that I will not change my mind about my faith. I have had to fight for my faith all my life and will never give it up. My dad passed away the year after my initial conversion, six months after I went into Bible College.

My dad taught his family explicitly that we should be independent thinkers, not obeying anyone, not needing any crutch, except of course the family itself. He said often that I was weak and that he was not pleased with my performance on this or that. He saw me as a weak person because I would not argue with him. I would not argue with him as a child. He told us that we needed to learn how to fight and not to trust any person ever, "not even your own ma or pa," were his words. My siblings and I were taught the ridiculous notion to "pull yourself up by your own bootstraps," as my dad had been taught by his parents.

I confronted my dad about abuse I had experienced as a child just simply saying to him, "Daddy I remember what happened to me as a child. I am going to leave your house for a while so I can get it together in my mind. I am going to work as a nurse in Corpus Christi. I love you, Daddy." He never said one word back to me. He did not say 'I love you' nor anything else to me that day. I left and never saw him alive again. He passed away two weeks later. I felt completely rejected by him. I was 37.

DID

I went into therapy at age 38 for Dissociative Identity Disorder, Post-traumatic stress disorder, and depression. Many people die with hopelessness in the midst of this disorder of DID, but I implore you, do not be one of them. There is so much to live for and so much life on the other side of the DID diagnosis. Remember you are not "a DID." You are not and never will be a "diagnosis." Following Jesus, doing my best to help others, and getting my mind off myself has been the best therapy. Worshipping the Lord Jesus has been so healing because, in his presence, we receive from God, our Healer. I glorify Jesus Christ as my Healer.

When I use the terms "wholeness," "wellness," "get well," or such, what I mean is moving toward integration, being fully functional in life, and participating in life. By "integration," I mean functioning within one united self without the inner conversation that can be so confusing. Integration can be a wonderful thing, but frankly, in the beginning it can be disturbing. It can be disturbing because we do not always want our parts to go away; we have become attached to them and their helpfulness to us, and it can seem "lonely" in the beginning with what seems like "no one to talk to." However, now is the time to start talking to other humans, real living people with whom you can be in relationship. Our Creator God made us to be in relationship—with Him and with others—and to love ourselves.

I firmly believe that healing cannot come without forgiveness of others because of the torment it causes us as individuals. We must work through all of our hurts though before we can fully forgive. We can stand bound in rage and fear for the rest of our life, or we can set ourselves free. "Fear involves torment . . ." (1 John 4:18). Forgiving a person does not mean that we go back and allow them to hurt us again.

Early in the year of my diagnosis, I heard in my inner self during prayer time the Scripture, "Beloved, do not think it strange concerning the fiery trial which is to try you, as though some strange thing happened to you, but rejoice to the extent that you partake of Christ's sufferings, that when His glory is revealed, you may also be glad with exceeding joy" (1 Peter 4:12-13). I was promised a fiery trial, but with joy following. And a fiery trial it was! In October of 1997, I was met with devastating diagnoses – Post-Traumatic Stress Disorder and Dissociative Identity Disorder. I was diagnosed with Major Depressive Disorder in 1992 at age 33.

As for DID, it is a greatly misunderstood phenomenon. "What is DID? DID is a little girl imagining that the abuse is happening to someone else."[26] I will explain this as it was explained to me. I have briefly explained "switching" parts. I will explain from my perspective what DID is, what it is good for, what it is not good for, and such. Briefly, it is a coping mechanism formed in the traumatized minds of young children. It happens much less frequently in adults because the trauma that it takes to create the disorder seems to be too much for the older human mind to cope with.

All "successful" DID persons are able to "go away" from the trauma in their mind, a kind of self-hypnosis, it seems to me.

---

[26] Colin Ross, *Dissociative Identity Disorder: Diagnosis, Clinical Features, and Treatment of Multiple Personality* (New York: John Wiley and Sons, Inc., 1997), 24.

When something really traumatic happens, the child "goes away," becoming someone else who can deal with the trauma temporarily. Self-hypnosis allows children to keep on being children and act somewhat normally during other times when they are not being abused. It allows those children to develop successful lifestyles as adults, often in professional careers. Though that person may not be particularly healthy emotionally, they have many resources to be successful in the world. The children that create an imaginary inner world are usually very intelligent, very creative, and have the capacity to learn. There is usually creative talent, either musical or artistic painting, drawing, or such. It is not simply when a child has an imaginary friend.

Parents need not worry if their young child, such as preschool age, has an imaginary friend. As the child grows older, the imaginary friend stage should cease. However, children with DID have many "imaginary friends" and "enemies" that are very real to them, actually parts of them. Sometimes children will let them be known to the outside world of their family or friends, but usually will not. Parents are typically involved in the cause if the child becomes dissociative, but this is not always the case. There are traumatic events that can happen without a parent's intent, but in cases of ongoing abuse, the parents' are most probably involved.

When there has been an unthinkable tragedy and the child does not know how to process this traumatic event, the human mind wants to try to make sense of the tragic event. The guilt automatically comes and the child thinks, "If only I had been better, this would not have happened. I must be bad." If this is not remedied, guilt and shame will set up camp, so to speak, within the child's soul and it will become a deep-seated internalized belief about them personally. They learn to think wonderful thoughts about their tormentors and bad thoughts about themselves. They learn to go somewhere else in their minds when bad things happen to good children. DID becomes a fantastic coping mechanism in the child and they can block out memories and hide them within their souls. These children can "see" themselves floating above their circumstances at times. DID gives false hope, but temporary relief.

As this occurs, certain brain changes occur. A part of the brain called the amygdala records traumatic events and these are replayed as movies throughout the lifetime, setting up all kinds of anxieties and phobias. Through teaching in therapy, people can change even the brain chemistry and set up new messages in the brain that tell a different story, a better story causing the self-esteem to return. This process requires a well-trained, skilled, and caring therapist, one sensitive to the patient, and many years of hard work for the patient. "A therapeutic relationship should include respect, information, connection, and hope (RICH)."[27] It may take some time to find the right therapist for the individual, but it is well worth the effort.

Though helpful to allow children to get through childhood and grow to adulthood, DID is not helpful in adult life. At a certain point around young to middle adulthood, coping begins to unravel and therefore life may begin to unravel also. If women are very secure in marriage and feel loved and cared for, often they do not lose coping. Women without these things do. Men lose coping, as well, being weighted down with the responsibilities of life and family.

Children with this phenomenon are tormented, have horrific nightmares many times, or night terrors. They may seem to be "psychic" children, seeing and hearing others. This is not childhood schizophrenia, though. This is almost the way it is portrayed in the movies, as the other and older term for this was Multiple Personality Disorder. But I am here to testify that people can and do get well and live normal lives; there are many therapists well trained to treat this disorder today as opposed to forty plus years ago when the first DID person came to the front. It is not hopeless; by no means is it hopeless, but it takes everything in a person to fight through this. A person must take ownership of their own healing process and work

---

[27] Laurie Ann Pearlman, Christine Courtois, *Relational Treatment of Complex Trauma*, Journal of Traumatic Stress, Vol. 18, No. 5, October 2005, 453.

with the person who helps them most. It takes the development of trust, sometimes for the first time in life.

So many times, people with this disorder will jump from therapist to therapist, pastoral counselor to pastoral counselor, and have guilt upon guilt piled on their heads in the process. It is not shameful to get psychological help from psychologists or psychiatrists, pastoral help from pastoral counselors, other trained therapists well versed in human behavioral theories, or from the multitude of counselors from Christian and other faith groups. It is this writer's opinion that a person must go wherever they need to go, drive wherever they need to drive, or move wherever they need to move to get the help they need. There could be no greater reason than personal healing to relocate if that becomes necessary. Most of all, one must never ever give up on themselves.

C.S. Lewis, the famous twentieth century Christian writer, had some things to say about psychoanalysis worthy of sharing here.

"Psychoanalysis itself, apart from all the philosophical additions that Freud and others have made to it, is not in the least contradictory to Christianity. Its technique overlaps with Christian morality at some points, and it would not be a bad thing if every *parson* [italics mine] knew something about it."[28] He tells the story of two men who went to war and were unable to commit to the fight due to fear. They were helped by psychoanalysis to overcome their fears and then had to make the decision whether or not to go back and fight or walk away taking care of himself and let other men fight the fight. [One soldier went back to do his duty and fight, the other made the choice to leave the battlefield and go home.] This is a moral choice.[29]

I have had a moral choice to make after my healing in the same way as the two men in the tale above. Would I live out my life living only for myself and my little family? Or would I use my healing for some good for others? It is my purpose to live to serve God and

---

[28] C.S. Lewis, *Mere Christianity* (New York: Macmillan Publishing Co, Inc., 1952), 84-85.
[29] Ibid.

others. I had to develop faith for it, though. I wondered for many years if I was well beyond help; for many years I questioned.

Bottom line with this diagnosis, I hoped that God was going to change me, but I even became unsure I wanted change at one point. It was terrifying. Remember, I had prayed for God to change me, begged Him to change me. He rarely ignores those kinds of prayers, but I almost changed my mind. I can remember for several years, I just wanted to die. I wanted God to take me out of here and take me on to eternity with Him, getting me out of the struggle of the cocoon in which He was placing me. Like a butterfly, He would not get me out of my struggle because to do so would make a crippled, deformed butterfly with broken wings. The struggle is God's way of creating a beautiful butterfly and a beautiful life. He wanted to give me wings to fly in this life as well as with Him for all eternity.

History

I got married at age nineteen after some years of rebellion against God with my boyfriend; it was not long into the marriage before I realized he was an angry man. He told me almost daily that he hated me and wished that I was dead. He struggled to win his parents' approval; they really liked me so he knew he could not leave me and win their approval. I guess the only other option of relief to him was if I died. We were married seven years and had two beautiful sons. I lived in fear and torment not knowing what my husband would do to me. He was emotionally and verbally abusive to me. I switched a great deal during these years because of hurt and fear. He called me a crazy loon and other names. After seven years, I got the courage to leave him, and we divorced. I had the knowing deep in my soul that if we did not get divorced someone would end up dead.

I remarried a few short months later; however, my second husband was an alcoholic with a lot of emotional problems. He had an abusive history and played it out with my family. His dad had shot him in the back when he was a teen and others abused him in other ways.

He pointed a gun at my little boys threatening to kill them when they were about four and six years old. I took the boys and left. I put my boys in psychotherapy for a time knowing that our lives were messed up by my husband. They did not consciously remember the abuse in the yellow house, but it came out in therapy. I really loved this man. We were both messed up emotionally and had a kindred spirit in one sense, but he tried to hurt those babies of mine, so I had to leave. I could not stay around and let them be destroyed. My second husband and I were divorced for several years, then he passed away of throat cancer. He came to know the Lord before his death and for this I am very thankful. My sons went with me to his funeral. I am so grateful to them for doing this for me.

I know now that God had been with me throughout my life for His reasons. I pray that I may be able to convince a teen or other young person not to make the same mistake I did, marrying too young and falling away from Christ because of turmoil within the church or within themselves. I would like teens that have been trained in the Word of God to believe what they have been taught, that God has inspired the Bible and has a reason for everything written there. He knows His creation. He knows what works, what does not work, what will bring us peace and comfort, and what will bring us misery. His rules are not there to prevent us from having a happy life, but to give us freedom in following Him. Life gets happier and more blessed the deeper one goes in obedience to Him. Even though our parents do not always do the right things in raising their children—I surely did not—God never fails us and always knows best.

Jesus Himself teaches that we are to be His hands and feet on earth. The words we should hear in heaven are, "Well done, good and faithful servant" (Matt 25:23), and "Come you blessed of My Father, inherit the kingdom prepared for you from the foundation of the world, for I was hungry, and you gave Me food; I was thirsty, and you gave Me drink; I was a stranger, and you took Me in. I was naked and you clothed me; I was sick, and you visited Me; I was in prison, and you came to Me . . . And the King will answer and say to them, Assuredly I say to you, inasmuch as you did it to one of the least of these My brethren, you did it to Me" (Matthew 25:34-36, 40).

Jesus said that His followers should be like Him and so many times, we are not. How tragic, how sad when you hear of great persons saying things like, "I like your Christ, I do not like your Christians. Your Christians are so unlike your Christ."[30] I strongly desire to be like Christ in all I do in hospital and other work. We must disciple our new converts and our established church members to strive to become more like Christ in all that they do.

The good news of Jesus is precious ointment to cure all ills. Through God's faithfulness and the faithfulness of many of His choicest servants, I have received that "medicine" and wish to pass it on. I have experienced the Lord's goodness and mercy because of the healing power of Jesus Christ in my life. "By the name of Jesus Christ of Nazareth . . . by Him, this [wo]man stands here before you whole" (Acts 4:10), integrated, integrative, and healed from the pain of the past, but knowing I will never want to stop growing and obtaining counsel, which I believe to be godly and wise.

The church can be a great support for hurting people or an agent to further hurt people. It depends on the character and personal demeanor of the ministers and members. Pastors can do much for their people by lending a listening ear, giving thoughtful prayers, and in a word "caring" for their congregation. Trauma is rampant in our culture. Various types of traumas exist; emotional, physical, sexual, spiritual, and verbal. The effects of these traumas are depression, anxiety, post-traumatic stress disorder, dissociative identity disorder, and other forms of mental illness and/or oppression. In Christ and with the help of the local church body and mental health professionals, women can find hope and healing. I am a woman so I feel I can speak for women on this issue, but I know there are many wounded men who need Christ and His church just as much.

---

[30] Quote by Mahatma Gandhi.

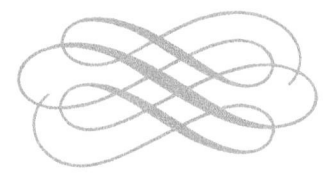

CHAPTER 3

EARLY POETRY

Out of the depths I have cried to You O Lord; Lord hear my voice!
(Psalm 130:1, 2a).

The Lord executes righteousness and
justice for all who are oppressed.
(Psalm 103:6).

During my years of self-searching through the therapy process, I expressed myself through poetry. Yes, self-searching had to happen, to be in self-reflection, to make peace with myself inside, and to reflect on memories.

Along my healing pilgrimage, poetry has become extremely important to me. I love to read poetry, hear poetry, but most of all I love to write it. I let go the depths of my emotions in my poetry. I wrote out of the pain, anguish, and turbulence in my soul. Out of the pain, I wrote poems that said everything I could not seem to say aloud. The poems seemed to progress through the years from darkest night to dawn as I experienced my "dark night of the soul."[31] My poems will be included along with the text of this book.

My poems might sound very childlike at times throughout this book. Often, I was in a child part when I wrote them, which explains why some sound rather simple, not what an educated person might write. However, education level has nothing to do with feelings, and all my poems are from feelings deep in my heart having true significance for me. My heart has become softened and tenderized, so much so that I step back and try to "toughen up" a bit at times.

My Song

My poem is my deep heart song
from a heart I thought so vile
it sings to me a lullaby
this hurting, wounded child

🦋🦋

These poems I wrote on my healing journey on what I consider the darkest day of my adult life, the day I attempted suicide. I call it simply "Poem."

Poem

Despised by God hated of man
    are the children
"The mother's" children slowly die
    always cry
        all alone
           and forever
        all alone

---

[31] St. John of the Cross, *The Dark Night of the Soul* (Whitefish, MT: Kessinger Publishing Co., 1995), first published in 1618.

never known
never understood
blown about in the wind
A tempest, the great storm of the ages

❧❧ ❧❧

"Poem" was written prior to my incident in the hospital where I found myself with a shower hose wrapped around my neck as a ligature hanging me, after having heard voices in my head shouting at me, "Die now! Hang yourself now!" These had been words spoken to me, which I internalized. It was a psychotic break. This was the only episode of a break in my life thankfully.

Attached to "Poem" are definitions I needed:[32]

Tempest = (a) a portion of time, a season, weather, storm. (b) an extensive violent wind, a furious storm. (c) Any violent tumult, to agitate.

Tumult = commotion or agitation of a multitude, usually with great uproar and confusion of voices. Violent agitation of the mind or feelings, a violent outburst. Turbulence combines with din.

Din = a. Loud noise, a welter of confused and discordant sounds, deafening uproar, clangor. b. To impress by insistent repetition, as "to din" a fact into his/her mind.

The above definitions almost define DID for me: Time lost, a storm, a furious storm, violent tumult of a multitude inside, confusion of voices, violent agitation of the mind, a welter of confused and discordant sounds, deafening clangor. I likened the sound in my head always to a symphony orchestra warming up, with all the musicians warming up their instruments at the same time, but not in harmony. In addition, while they are warming up, all the people waiting for the performance are trying to talk above the instruments in idle conversation. This leaves what I would best describe as a "welter of confused and discordant sounds." When I heard this in my head

---

[32] *Webster's Dictionary 1987 Edition* (Miami: P.S.I. & Associates, Inc., 1987).

constantly, it was a deafening clangor for sure. I had gone to the symphony many times as a child, so this is where I got the analogy. The voices were not from the outside of me but in my head.

The Scream

at the injustice
at the loss of time
at the betrayal of those closest
raw emotion
no violence, just screaming from the inner being
coming clean for once in life
coming from all inside
    safety
    fear is gone
    catharsis
    much healing
        happiness, joy and freedom
        await …
            on the other side of The Scream

❧ ☙

This poem was written after I was given a safe place to scream in my therapist's office. Nothing happened, no one locked me up, and no one died or even got hurt that day, the day I began to lose my fear of my own anger. After the day I wrote "Poem," I was not hospitalized again; that was my second and final hospitalization. I wanted to stay out of the hospital. The incident that prompted that was the only suicide attempt I ever made and it was a strange circumstance. I feared too much what God might do to me if I committed suicide. I did not believe I would have gone to heaven if I had. I credit God Himself for saving me and keeping me away from hospitalization again.

The Wilderness of None

Out in the wilderness of none
   there is no answer
      no rationality
         no causality
            no mentality

I was given no thought
   no time
      no touch

empty – sad – lonely
   wilderness

wandering in that wilderness
   reactive wandering
   restless wandering
   relentless wandering

it is an empty place – a void
     in time

wretched wandering
woeful wandering
weary wandering
out in the wilderness of none

     no mercy
     no love
     no compassion
     no care
     nothing there
     nothing shared
     at least not with me
     nothing but hate

I was the bait
at the gate

To the wilderness of none …

❧ ❧

In the Silence

What happens in the silence?
what speaks? what is seen?
what is felt, tasted, smelled?
rotting flesh, electric shocks felt
spiders and more creepy crawlers crawling
commands to "Hang!"
Silence kills.

❧ ❧

I really believed back then that silence kills, that if the noise died, I would die. However, having extraneous noise around me was too much for my overloaded brain to bear. There was so much noise in my head that television or radio was too much, so I kept my home silent while I was healing. I relished the silence even after I got to a certain place of healing. It remains extremely healing to be in the silence today, not because I am still hearing noise in my head, but because it is so peaceful now. I know that some people who have healed from DID have to have noise around them all the time, such as the radio or television. They seem to perpetuate the noise they always heard inside. This does not make much sense to me because now that my head is silent, I love silence.

I love peace and tranquility that comes from inner quiet. I know that we are all different, though, so I respect others' opinions. For me, silence is a wonderful gift of healing. I can now go hiking and enjoy the calm and quiet sounds of nature. I can actually hear the birds singing and the leaves rustling, which is wonderful to me. These early times of poem writing, though, were filled with despair. The next poem is probably the most despairing poem I wrote. It tells of the depth of my inner turmoil. It is; however, very meaningful to me even in the despairing.

White Doves Rage

white doves rage in a tornadic storm
the winds they whip in cyclonic form
torture and torment at every turn, turns up the heat, the voltage, the burn
beating down walls of angry resistance
roaring as a hurricane of raging insistence
only the fury of doves could be described, by tiny souls torn in the struggle to survive
blood pours down in the rhythm of pain
little ones gone never hearing the refrain, of their own song within them, why them, why?
--fly into oblivion at the sound of their cries
bleeding hearts silenced in the cold still earth
never again knowing a heart's joy and mirth
and those left behind with crushed spirits, laid bare
sounds of their mournful melodies haunting the air
white doves cry a rainstorm of shame
a deluge of terror calls each one by name
some forced to go, some forced to stay, how can we understand heaven's way
the ones left behind cry still yet today, why must they live in this tormented way
fighting for life they lived, but why did they fight
better it seems to go to the wind, the depths, or fiery red heights
anywhere but here in the rhythm of pain

gone from the sorrowful personal disdain, of what I had to do to
survive
how can I forgive my desperate drives
seeing flashes of hurt and grief, agony and shock
the dove fights for life screaming malicious malevolent talk
the dove once so white, so soft, so sweet, pure innocence now hides
in her shadowy retreat, white dove calls through
misty black night, relentless, helpless wails of fright
white wings pinned with little breathing room
deep in the fog of the marsh of gloom
sadistic cruel minds twist yarns of madness
threatening cruel death or perpetual sadness, for all time and eternity
would they succumb to lost hope, would they perish, once fragile
hearts broken like glass
hated so badly when they should have been cherished
silver strands of crimson hate
twist the cords of elusive fate
winnowing illusion of redeeming flight
a white dove reverie into haunted black night

❧ ❧

When white doves rage, it is a very unnatural phenomenon. Doves
denote peace and tranquility, calm, serenity, and placid solitude. Doves
are a biblical symbol of the divine, the Holy Spirit of God. White
is the color of purity, cleanliness, clarity, chastity, and innocence.
Rage is a strong emotion, out of control anger, a tempest as a great
storm within a human being.

All is not right with the world if white doves are raging. It is not
the way it was intended; it is bizarre, troubled, and disturbed. Life
is too precious to let it wither away in that sense. Innocent children
must be protected. When working with the pregnancy centers doing
sonography, I was heartbroken at all of the killing of the innocents.
This had a part in this poem as well. God has a plan and a purpose
for every human being and life begins at conception. God can change

the flight pattern of the dove and though she does not fly high, she learns to fly free of her caged encumbrances.

The above poem is one expression of the agony and torment in my soul and mind that I have carried throughout my life. It speaks of the humiliation and insanity of childhood abuse of all kinds and the killing of the innocents by abortion. It was totally unthinkable that the nightmare was real. I struggled to keep my head above water, so to speak. Insanity tried to take me, but it could not. God's got me!

My Rage

I am a storm brewing in the distance, soon all may see,
what is brewing is the tempest, deep inside of me,
I will rage through the secrets, I will rage through the pain,
I will rage all through life, am I insane?
they thought they had me, they thought they had won,
they beat me down, I had nowhere to run,
I raged in the silence, I raged in the pain, I raged in the storm another depressing refrain,
the tempest it broke me, for once they shall see all,
the truth inside of me, ashamed I did fall,
the storm clouds were broken, by those evil, cruel men,
they rendered me silent, they said I could never win,
however even in the quiet, I marched on in my fight,
they thought I gave up, but oh no not quite!
I raged when they hurt me, I raged blaringly, loudly, I raged quietly softly, I raged silently, proudly … but I did rage …
until the light broke the night.

Brook Sea Raven

Brook Sea Raven flies free
once cursed as a demon child
lies dispelled
the wound broke open
release of purulent poison
putrid purpura once festered and bleeding
now trickles and ebbs a healing flow
cleansing the agony
washing the pain away
her true identity revealed
a God-child, a loved child
Sea Raven's new wings flutter
lifting off to peaceful dawn
over a tranquil sea

Torrent of Abuse

all-encompassing torrent, raging rapids,
healing for the waterfall cliff,
to plummet headlong into the dark abyss,
fire and water, wind and stone, thunder and hail,
an approaching hurricane of terror,
suddenly water calms -winds cease -miracle comes -love heals
healing is true, finally free to spread her wings,
upward to the heavens, the torrent flies away like a bird

Dark Days of Old

In days gone by, dark days of old, days of my repeated vexations, disquieting unsettling disturbing, days of my tormented wanderings, the sea alone was more restless than my troubled soul, waves crashing against the rocky shore, in tumultuous dissonance, the sea tames the restlessness in me.

The Train

my heart is headed for a train wreck wreaking havoc on my soul
the train is headed down the tracks of destruction, derailment,
dissociation, disintegration, death – or worse ...
slamming out of control ready to careen off the mountain
"that's what happens to little bad children ... off the mountain!
off the mountain you go!"

I awake knowing my train wreck has come
I heard the signals, felt the fire, saw the terrors
I will never be the same
unable to move, unable to breathe
unable to die, unable to live
Never the same, never ever the same.

Why?

Why?
There are no easy answers
No! there are no answers at all

Depraved manhood – degenerate womanhood
I was asked, "What happened to gentle womanhood?"
I answered, "It was crushed by cruel manhood!"
or so I would have answered, but I thought too late.
Why do I still seek an answer when there is none?
It is like spraying a water gun on my forest fire of rage,
or like giving a sugar pill to a corpse –
the corpse of my sadness.

Grief persists
Tears stagnate – unable to be expressed
Sadness stymied
The corpse remains – for now.

Smoke Rises

smoke rises from the burning furnace of my
dreams, dreams about my family.
bad choices? wrong choices?
what does it matter now?
relationship dreams scorched, charred and
lying in the rubble of the Ground Zero[33]
of my heart.

Grief

grief is an old house full of cobwebs.
we walk through and wonder,

---

[33] "Ground Zero" refers to the site of the twin towers in New York City after the terrorist attack of 9/11/2001.

"when will a spider emerge to bite us?"
"is it safe?" we ask.
"not usually," it is told.
"not for long anyway ..."
wearily we wander through that old house
of emotion
when will the spider return?
when will the spider return?

Soul Aches

in quiet desperation
I fade and fall
bad, sad, mad
weak in my body
resolute in my will
my soul aches
hungry for touch

The following is a poem about my story written later in 2001. It shows hope, the beginning of precious hope.

Climbing my Mountain

I feel like a mountain climber ...
Here I am, climbing a very high mountain, holding tightly to the rope, my lifeline.
I am holding onto it tightly with all my might, climbing, climbing, climbing, out of

Childhood, slowly, slowly but surely, realizing it is difficult to keep holding that rope through this portion of the climb.

I am very tired but making some headway up the mountain. Now, I climb through Adolescence, sweating profusely holding on with all my might. I feel I may pass out any minute. However, I see that I am halfway up this mountain now.

Turning back is no option; I have come this far. I feel the sweat on my back until I think I will dehydrate and die, but I am holding tight to that lifesaving rope.

I continue to climb slowly upward, into a hopeful, yet fearful time, struggling toward
Young Adulthood, what a stressful, busy time to be in. I am very tired, fatigued, and do not know how much longer I can go on, but on I go.

At this point, I cannot look down, I cannot look back or I will fall back. I know that my own age, Middle Adulthood, is at the top of the mountain. Can I face it? At the top are wholeness, integration, and wellness.

I am three-quarters of the way up, but I feel my weakness, my fatigue, my human frailty. Where do I get the needed energy to make it "over the top" when it seems all my energy is spent?

By the way, how have I made it this far up, when I believed I could not? It is live or die time, in this climb, no net to catch me if I fall!

But, oh, I remember something—yes, there is a net! How could I have forgotten? The safety net is the loving arms of my Father God.

I let myself be totally dependent on Him now because I am so weak and I realize; yes, I climbed this mountain, so far, but not by myself. Not alone! Never all alone anymore, ever again!

I feel the arms of my Lord and Savior, Jesus Christ lifting me higher and higher, as though I am being catapulted to the top; not only to the top, but up and over the top. Jesus has big, strong arms and I declare my complete dependence on Him! I must; therefore, "Trust in the Lord with all [my] heart and lean not on [my] own understanding. In all [my] ways I will acknowledge Him, and He shall direct [my] paths" (Proverbs 3:5, 6).

I do not have an anthropomorphic view of God. I know that God is Spirit, the Holy Spirit, and that He does not have literal arms, hands, and feet except in the Person of Jesus Christ when He walked the earth, now the only Man who is in heaven. Therefore, these metaphors are simply my human way of drawing comfort from God.

After I fully integrated, I felt I had a lot of catching up to do. I went into years of life therapy. I needed to learn to relate to people in different ways, develop new coping mechanisms, and think differently in many situations. DID was all I had ever known and it definitely was not working for me anymore.

My poetry and thought certainly took a turn toward hope and self-love a few months following my suicide attempt in the hospital.

Going Seaside

I am like so many others
in a sea of survivors
so many faces
of anguish, of pain, of torment
then of relief, help, and hope
they did not count on us
did they?

The Garden

come as you are, come on in
come on into the garden inside
it is cozy and beautiful inside
and you all deserve to be here
in the garden
so please, come on in

❧❧

Scripture Meditation

Holy Bible
Isaiah 58:11
"The Lord will guide you continually
And satisfy your soul in drought.
And strengthen your bones,
You shall be like a watered garden,
And like a spring of water,
Whose waters do not fail."

❧❧

To Know You

Lord, please allow me to know You,
        really know You,
allow me to love You,
        really love You.
allow me to trust You,
        really trust You.
So that I can join You where You are working now,
open my eyes to see where You are working now

Lord, I want to work for You,
Lord, I want to work with You,
Lord, I want to love You will all my heart,
and most of all be found together with You.

Love,
Me

Glitter on the Ground

there is glitter on the ground
right outside my threshold
God has made it a gorgeous show
with all its glittering silver and gold
and shiny lights called winter snow
oh so beautiful to behold
the crown of winter on earth below
no beauty does He withhold
amazing spectacle, awesome glow.

December Rose

frail little flower
or
determined with all her might,
to grow
in spite
of
circumstances given her
new growth
springs forth in winter

I wrote "December Rose" at the same time as "Glitter," when the southern autumn had been quite warm and an unexpected turn of weather caused a surprising snow to fall. There was a single rose on the bush just outside my back door. I pondered the beauty of that little red rose and took it as an analogy of my life and healing. I wrote the poems in this chapter eight years prior to the "Later Poetry" of Chapter 14. During that interim, I became fully integrated, integrative, and continued post-integration therapy to learn new life skills.

This is the final alteration to the poem "December Rose," at one time the symbol for my hope. "Hope deferred makes the heart sick, but when the desire comes, it is a tree of life" (Proverbs 13:12). The hope in my heart was the desire for wholeness and a normal life, a successful life in God's plan. I did not know what that meant exactly, to be in God's plan, but now I know I am in the center of His plan. Living His plan is the only way I can live a "normal" life.

December Rose

frail little flower
or
determined with all her might

to grow
in spite of circumstances given her

snow petals fall
upon her crimson face

snow-capped flower
winter's chill upon her soul

Life
in the midst of death

new growth springs forth in winter
Hope has bloomed!

Shattered Pieces

shattered pieces of my broken life
is there any relief from
my restlessness and strife

shattered pieces once all in disarray
formed many questions in my mind including
who am I, I pray?

my heavenly Father told me who
I am He said I belong to Him
if this be true and I know it is
my soul is satisfied ever again

In Pieces

shattered dreams
shattered soul
as
shattered china
fine china

Death of a Dance

it is a death of hope

death of a dream
death of my love
but I must lean on my Love, my Father
my God.
In this life I danced with my love,
a painful dance at times.

now in this life I dance with my Love
the dance of joy and peace.
and I will dance again
and forever.

The Rose of Love

A rose I gave to my one fair love
it was red and new
A tiny flower of love from above
symbol of love so true
I went to see him one last time
to give my gift of love
I longed to hold him like before
time stood still, "O my dove!"
I left the rose on his precious heart
though my own heart was breaking
For his eyes had closed their one last time
faint was my heart and aching
The rose will forever be with him
as he will be with me
the rose is my heart for us to share
until eternity

It brought me great comfort to know that my second husband had accepted Jesus Christ as Lord prior to his death and with this; I have hope of seeing him again in heaven.

Together

I went to that place before with him
"This is where they will plant me someday"
And together we will be again
sometime, somewhere, someway

I will Dance with Him

my Jesus asked to dance with me
and of course, I said I would
it thrilled my heart so much much more
than anything ever could.

this came at a time when the sky went dark
when the grief was too much to bear
the world was no longer a lovely place with
my love no more I would share.

God turned my grief to calm delight
as dance with Him I did
I know I am loved beyond any doubt
til this earth farewell I bid.

I'll dance with Him forever
forever in His care
meanwhile I will go with Him
follow Him anywhere.

He Told Me

My Jesus loves me so so much
He told me and it's true
I believe Him, oh I believe Him
I believe Him through and through.

But You Said

but you said you loved me
but how could you really?
you had nothing to give
but pain
you received pain I know
but why did you give it
so liberally?
why couldn't you turn
away from the pain
and love us?
all I wanted was to love you
and ease your pain
how I tried too,
and that's why
your betrayal hurt more
than almost anything else
in my life,
I believed in you.

What – Where?

What would I do without him?
  now that I have found him
     I don't know

What would my love-struck, love-starved
  love-seared soul do cry live die
     I don't know

Waves crashing against an eroded shore
         beaten
            down
              again
Where is hope, my love
  two souls walking in a non-illumined forest
    through a dark mist
      an opaque veil
        I don't know
We surrender ourselves to fear to tears to Love

Hope - Light - Love

    I wrote a poem about my adventures in travel across the world. All through my life, poetry has been a passion for me. The poem tells of some of my most memorable places, the hardest places.

Asian Nights

Asian nights of mystery and danger
Beautiful night lights of gold and blue

Glow like Christmas lights across the shepherd's fields
Trekking across deserts beyond human limits
Sounds of war raging across borders sealed.

The hope of new lands
New cultures, new mother tongues
New people to love
Let it be so.

Exciting to me these new exotic places
Where real people live real lives
Turbulent, terrifying lives
New and different to me yet weighty are the needs
Little Asian children work on the streets to survive.

My heart bleeds
My passion soars.

Hot dusty roads of an Asian jungle
Cobras lurking in the shadows
Darkness and danger, pestilence and pain
Death and destruction
Light again.

New adventures
New highs
New beauty and wonder.

No humdrum life for me
What a marvelous adventure, a privilege
Traveling roads, lonely roads
Sad roads of sad bad history
Life has been hard in godless abodes.

My heart bleeds
My passion soars.

Depressed roads, heart wrenching roads
Roads of excitement
In new lands and old from sea to shining sea
Lonely pilgrims in futile labors
Struggling to live and go where they are free.

New adventures
New highs
New beauty and wonder.
The hope of even new lands
New cultures, new mother tongues
New people to love
O let it be so.

I wrote many poems during my time of chaplain training in the hospital. It was a time of great reflection on my life and a restructuring of myself for service. I dealt with previously crippling emotions and did sometimes seemingly impossible tasks of working with people when I felt quite crippled and stifled emotionally. I kept doing the work in spite of my feelings, which taught me a lot about ministering to others. Our supervisor sent us on poem workshops, which enhanced my desire to write poems to reflect and extract deep emotions within.

When Someone Deeply Listens to Me

when someone deeply listens to me
it is like sitting by a cool mountain brook
tender sounds on the stones
in the refreshing mountain air
nowhere to have to go, no time constraints
gentle breeze blowing by
O' so gentle and sweet

tender whispers of dew on my face
a rare gift
so rare, so beautiful, so tender

What Will Happen If I Am Bold?

What will happen if I am bold?
will the sky fall?
will fire become ice?
will light become dark?
will day become night?
will the world stop on its axis?
will they fire me, sell me?
humiliate me, eat me, kill me?

I found my voice. I really found my voice for the first time in my life when I was heard for the first time by one who cared. When this happened, I was deeply moved.

When I Am Heard

When I am heard,
It is:
Fireworks, Fiesta, Fulfillment

It is like fireworks bursting beautiful
in the darkened sky

Celebration
Hope

Peace
Overcoming

It is like a fiesta of color in my soul,
my soul's delight

Celebration
Hope
Peace
Overcoming

It is fulfillment knowing
my bonds are cut,
my bounds are clear,
and
my burdens are carried away

Here is another of my devotional poems to God. These poems
were written by the Christian "ones" of me, and were a testimony
to the others then too wounded to trust in anyone, even God.

Wholly Holy

my Lord my God
You are in glory awesome
You are profound, great, complicated – yet love but simple me

You are wholly awesome
You are the holy only God
I love You so
and I know You love me too
You are mine and I belong to You
I see Your face

in all its glorious radiance
this is my hope, the hope of all my life

Poetry has been a safe outlet of expression for my deepest, darkest moments in life. It takes on a life of its own. Poetry for me has evolved into a means of expressing devotion to God, of expressing my deepest thoughts and emotions, and to wonder at God's amazing creation. The wonder of His creation is fascinating. Poems are a way to cope with the pain and to come to a better self- understanding as well. As a child, I wrote a few poems about certain ceremonious events, such as birthday celebrations and the like, but never dared to write about my pain. Thankfully, this has changed in my adult life as I reclaimed an artistic part of myself.

First, I wrote poems at the most painful times in my adult life, remembering past pain. Later, I wrote poems at the wonderment and worship of God. Still later, poems gave expression to my thoughts and feelings concerning my work in ministry. Latest, I have written joyful poems as I have retaken joy, peace, and love back into my life. Also in the poetry are seen concurrent emotions; my mind fluctuated between parts and is reflected herein. Some poems were written to God, some about God, some hopeful, but many hopeless. I found I went through a plethora of emotions during these very turbulent years in which I found myself. This is the way I felt for so long when I was going through therapy, those long hard days wondering if it was all worth the effort I was putting out? Yes, it certainly was!

Here are a few more poems that I found that I had written several years ago, which were personal prayers and devotions to God. These were and still are very special to me along my healing path. I call them my letters to Jesus.

Letters to Jesus

Jesus My Treasure

Dear Lord, I pray for the grace to do Your will every day of my life, and that Your grace may never run out. You are my Love, my Treasure. "I rejoice at Your Word as one who finds great treasure."[34]

His answer: Immeasurable grace, I have immeasurable grace, My child, all sufficient grace for you. "And He said to me, 'My grace is sufficient for you, for My strength is made perfect in weakness.'"[35]

Love, God

Love for You

My love for You Lord
Burning bright
Hearts aglow
Full of Light
Hope rekindled
God's delight

My Shield

There is none more worthy of my devotion than You Lord.
I live for the pleasure of Your will,

---

[34] Psalm 119:162.
[35] 2 Corinthians 12:9.

by Your grace alone.
I am kept by Your Holy Spirit,
"sealed for the Day of Redemption" (Ephesians 4:30).
I give You thanks, You alone are worthy, You said,
"I am your Shield, your exceedingly great reward" (Genesis 15:1)

❧❧❧

Christmas Gifts for You

O my Lord God, Jesus, I want to bring Christmas gifts to You,
I want to bring You the Gold of my obedience to the works of Your will,
and not my own; to be tried in Your Refiner's fire.

I want to bring You Myrrh[36] so that the pain I have caused You by my
bitter sin would be removed.

I want to bring You Frankincense[37] to be white in purity so as to bring
You the perfume of a sweet spirit toward You. O Lord let it be so.

❧❧❧

I was praying and pondering how much of my life seemed wasted
to me because of all the times I had not thought of how my sin hurts
Jesus. I did not really begin to heal from the effects of the abuse that
caused DID until I let go of self-pity, forgot about myself, and sought
to minister to Jesus and others. It is amazing what a difference this
made in my life.

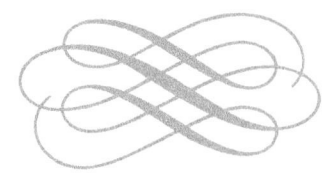

CHAPTER 4

PILGRIMS ALL

Teach me Your way, O Lord, I will walk in Your
truth. Unite my heart to fear Your name.
(Psalm 86:11).

Behold You desire truth in the inward parts, and in the
hidden part You will make me know wisdom.
(Psalm 51:6).

The Scriptures above are important to me and to everyone who ventures on the journey of healing from DID. Sometimes it is difficult to "see" the old stuff and "make straight paths," but the only way out is through the "stuff," looking closely to dispel lies. I tell my story of how I made my way out, and if it helps even one person, my efforts will be worthwhile. I have changed the names in this chapter for protection of sensitive inward parts.

In this chapter, I will name each part of myself that helped me cope with my life and describe its function. When I was first diagnosed, it all seemed very surreal and it took time to come to grips with all this, to believe what was happening to me, and to learn how I had structured my inner world. I did not want to refer to different aspects of myself as "parts" because it sounded like dead body parts to me. As time went on, though, it was just easier and I got past the "body parts" analogy. I no longer thought of them as "dead." Sometimes they are referred to as "parts" or "alters," I mostly call them "parts."

Now I realize that there are not *parts* to anyone's soul, that this is a matter of personal perspective. We are one person with three aspects: body, soul, and spirit. Some would argue that we are simply beings with two parts, body and spirit/soul, but it is easier for me to think of a human person as body, soul, and spirit with the body being the physical part of the person. The soul consists of mind, will, and emotions, and the spirit is the part of the person that belongs to God that no other can touch or kill. The spirit is God's and will live forever with Him if the person has received Him as Lord and Savior. My perception of my soul was shattered or fractured.

To each person with DID, there are common threads. One thread is the "system map." It is the way of thinking about the whole self. Some people see the map as a group of actors in a play, some see it as a road map on the road of life, and some see it as a house or mansion. There are as many different ways to see a "system map" as there are people. All of us who are affected by DID have one, but it takes time to come to grips with this fact, and to recognize it. When I was a child, my family did genealogy. My paternal grandfather's family came from Germany, while my paternal grandmother's family came from England. My maternal grandmother's family came from England, while my maternal grandfather's family came from Scotland.

My mother's mother, whom I called Mama, my primary caregiver, took me everywhere with her. We visited relatives all over the area where we lived and interviewed many people for her written genealogy that she worked on all my childhood up to her death. I knew a lot about our family history.

Mama spoke of England often. She spoke of how the family came over from England three generations before. She spoke with a light British accent and was most proud of her mother's side of the family, from England. I learned how to speak the way she did. Four years ago, when I returned from a trip to the Middle East, we stopped in England for a day and a half. As we returned on the airplane, I began to speak this way without my awareness. An American that sat by me asked where in England I was from and when I said I am an American, she did not believe me. This was actually scary to me that I could sound that authentic, having never lived there. It had been an automatic response to being immersed in the culture even for a day. I had to consciously drop the accent and begin to speak the way I normally do now.

In a child with DID, there is a different part assigned to each function that a child needs to perform. If a child needs to be strong for some particular reason, there is a part for that. If the child needs to play in a certain way or with certain other children, there is a part for that. If the child needs to cry and be soft, there is a part. If the child needs to get mad without losing control, there is a part, and the list goes on. There are "triggers" that happen, a certain sound, for example, or a certain person's cues when that person is aware of the system. Many of the adults in these children's lives know the system and often have implemented the whole process.

A bell, the sound of a phone ringing, the sound of a dog barking, of a baby crying, and a host of other common sounds can provide triggers. Many times, people do or say things that trigger the child but have no idea they are doing the trigger. Many triggers are built into the system, mostly common sounds or words, to ensure that the system goes on uninterrupted. Those triggers remain throughout life until the system is brought down into the consciousness through trained professional help.

Do not try this alone! I am fully convinced that God put other people into our lives to help us. People have died trying to help and heal themselves in the circumstances of this disorder. People have died both accidentally and due to suicide because the pressure became too much; life seemed too difficult to live. Please, my dear friend, do not harm yourself. There is hope out here; there is healing! You can learn to live again and love the life you make for yourself.

The definition of "pilgrim" is "a person who journeys to a sacred place for religious reasons."[36] They have journeyed to the sacred space inside of me. They all belong with me forever and I love them dearly. I just no longer refer to them as separate names; all of them are me. I honor myself and my system for protecting me and helping me cope. I will now go on to explain the phenomenon that was DID for me. Please meet the pilgrims in my land.

The leader of my system was Paul, a boy who is strong and able to take care of "us." He is physically strong and when I needed to be strong, I "called on" Paul to help me be strong. It worked. He is also strong in spirit, never weak, never cried at the dinner table when being yelled at, but when I was at the table, he was never "out." The weak ones took over. The weak ones took over because submission was the only safe way to cope with my dad.

Susy is a toddler about two years old who has no feelings and stays very quiet. She is a protector, as well, by her silence. Sissy is a four-year old who is scared all the time, who was manipulated to "kill the monster." Carol is the eight-year-old, the playful one. She is strong and loves to play "boy" games like football, kickball, basketball, and Red Rover. She is a tomboy, and is a good friend of Paul, the strong boy. Carol was very unhappy, very sad when she was told that she could no longer play "boy" games outside but had to stay inside because she was a girl.

Boy parts in a girl's system do not necessarily mean that girl is homosexual or vice versa. It really has nothing to do with sexual orientation; it is a matter of function. It is simply awareness that there is a lack of safety and girls are socialized to believe they need male strength; at least we were back when this was happening to me in the 1960s. The same holds true for girl parts in a boy's system; simply the need for tenderness and care are there that may be lacking in the boy, as strength may be lacking in the girl.

Before I go on, I will say that there are some parts that like one another, and others that hate one another, and everything in between. This is where self-loathing can come in. One part clings on

---

[36] *Webster's Dictionary.*

to a negative statement made by a parent and believes only this until "convinced otherwise." A parent may say, "You will never amount to anything" and that part takes that to the greatest extreme and learns to sabotage the whole system to reinforce that what that parent says is true, "because, of course, parents know everything." The children do not blame parents. If this were the case, who would feed and clothe the child, how would the child survive? In the child's eyes, they would not, so they take the blame on themselves, the safest option. The child is riddled with guilt. They see themselves as a bad person.

In later therapy, these "rules" can slow the recovery process when sabotage is happening every time the person makes a move toward recovery. Some people have more sabotage in them than others, it seems, but sabotage is common to all the ones I have known that were affected by DID.

In my situation, and therefore in my system, I found it quite unsafe to get angry. People did not survive when they talked back to the "masters" or went "out of control" in arguing. Therefore, I had five parts to control my anger. These were all male parts. Girls were not supposed to get angry, so to cope with this human emotion, I had to turn to male counterparts. I called the five, "the Fight Team." The names were Jesse, Bruce, Trouble, Kill You, and Billy Boy. The way it worked was that if I got a little angry, Jesse would come out and the anger was mild and controlled. If mild anger did not work and there was a continued perceived threat to me, the anger would escalate. If I got a little angrier, Bruce would come out and do something physical, like crush a flower or hit a wall or a pet. The third level of anger was for Trouble, who would fight and fight to protect the body. Trouble would scream/yell as a means of an attempt to intimidate the enemy. This was the part that screamed at "the monster." If there was the need to continue from here, for added protection, Kill You would come out. Kill You was the one who killed "the monster." Then at the end of the scenario, Billy Boy would cry in shame and take on all the guilt of my whole person, all the guilt of killing, and any guilt left over from any other incident.

When I say, "come outside" I mean that the part is present and up front to perform their particular job. After their job is done, they "go back in" to hide, unperceived by others until their job is again necessary for survival. There is "amnesia" in most cases, at least when the person is still a child and the parts do not know each other's functions, or even that there is anyone else around at times when they do not feel safe. Sometimes there is some knowing about "others," but the parts become imaginary friends in order to protect the child from being labeled as crazy by a teacher or other adult who knows nothing of the child's inner world. A caring teacher might want to point out to a parent that the child may need some help in the professional counseling world or some other such help. This is not what the parent of this child wants to hear, so many checks and balances are placed into the system for prevention of these events.

My mother never denied anything that I told her that were memories. And she apologized to me for not protecting me when I was a child. Most people do not get to receive the gift of hearing "I am sorry for hurting you," or "I'm sorry for not protecting you," neither do they get to be validated that what all they believe is true. These two facts helped me greatly in having the courage to write this book. I want to make it clear, however, that just because the person with DID does not get validation or an apology from a parent, it does not mean that the events did not happen; you can trust yourself and your memories.

Here, I will make a list of my system participants. I am a list-maker; I keep myself organized this way. I am happy to introduce my "pilgrims in the land of I."

1. Paul = the eight-year-old leader of the pack, the strong boy who takes care of everyone
2. Sissy = the four-year-old scared little girl who cries everywhere she goes, very sweet to everyone, gets manipulated a lot
3. Carol = the eight-year-old who is strong and loves to play, we call on her when it is time to have fun, always happy

4. Jesse = one of the fight guys, a boy about six years old, who is a little bit angry

5. Bruce = one of the fight guys, a boy about five years old, who is a little bit angrier

6. Trouble = one of the fight guys, a boy about three years old, who is even angrier and throws temper tantrums to try to protect everyone

7. Kill You = one of the fight guys, a boy of four years old, who gets so angry that he kills when he has to, when he has to "kill or be killed," as he was threatened, though he would never choose to, and only when pushed to these great extremes

8. Billy Boy = the last of the fight guys, a boy of four years old who takes on all the guilt of the system, equalizes the system by crying, repenting and turning from the murderous ways every time

9. Bambi = the "sexy little girl," a six-year-old who does what she has to do, she later grows to be about seventeen years old, always sexual and called sexual nicknames, likes sex very much and carries much shame because she does. She also has fantasized of every form of sexual perversion

10. Amy = the little girl, about six, who is rival to Bambi and tattles on her, she has no friends, she does not like anyone and no one likes her, she antagonizes everyone, often calls Bambi bad names

11. Miss T = the name of a part of unknown age who is always in the way or doing something to cause trouble for others, messes everything up when things are going well, probably a nickname for Miss Trouble

12. Sissy May = mother's favorite child, about six years old, the spoiled child who tells everyone she is mother's favorite, though she really is not, mother wants people to believe she is spoiled because of all the wonderful things mother does for her, it is a lie; she obeys "the mother" no matter what

13. Rosemarie = the "little nurse" who is three years old when she begins to take care of mother when she has her "sick

headaches." Mama says she must take care of mother, hold her head with a cold cloth while she throws up, and empty her throw up pan. Rosemarie must wash mother in bed, and take care of her without ever moving or touching the bed. The mother yells at her abusively all the while she is trying to help her

14. May Elizabeth = the little religious girl who is always good, always religious, the church musician, an excellent musician

15. I = the core person that exists, but never really knew what to call her, I just knew she is female because the body is female, a "safe name" because everyone says I

16. Martha = a two-year-old child who is dead inside and can endure any and all pain

17. Gregory = the informer of the system, tells secrets between parts when needed, is a helper when healing time comes around and promotes co-consciousness, seems to know all the stories

18. Susy = two-year-old girl with no feelings, somewhat like Martha

❦❦❦

One very important rule of any system is that you never tell your name when you are in your role. It is never safe to tell your name. If you tell your name, the abusers can take advantage of you and curse you. The abusers can then find your people and do unspeakable things. Because it is never safe to say one's name, one learns immediately to forget their name. When they are pressured or interrogated, they will never remember their true name.

The person may give a different name without any awareness that it is not the truth because, for them at the time, it is truth. It is not a lie to the person when they give a different name because they truly believe what they say. This is a strong rule and even in therapy when they believe themselves to be in a safe place, they will not remember their own name because it is simply too dangerous. They have been betrayed and threatened too many times; no one can take that chance again. The person may resort to telling a lie if they are in a perceived life-and-death situation. Many children with DID learn to tell lies often to protect themselves from perceived exile, cruel punishment, and/or perceived death, which is a coping mechanism that needs to change when healing occurs and we learn new life skills. The child's whole life has been about perceived survival. They feel they may die though this may not be a reality.

The core host is the true original person born in the body. Most of the time in DID, it is very confusing who that core host really is. We tend to think that the part that is out at the time is the core host person, which I will now refer to only as "the core." The core is the person who existed before the abuse. If the abuse happened first at age eight, then that person will be intact and known. If the abuse started when the person was two years old or so, or any age before conscious memory begins in that child, the core will be unknown. Sometimes the core is revealed to the person, but many times it is not. It is not imperative to know this information, though it is extremely satisfying for the person when they can have some idea of when the abuse began and when they were "innocent." Sadly, some children never were innocent in their lifetime; they were abused or neglected from earliest infancy, but they were innocent in the sight of the true God.

Sometimes when a DID person is cursing God, they are merely cursing a person who misrepresented themselves as God to them, an actor pretending to be God, which is actually quite common. At other times, the person may be cursing the true God Himself, but as I said, God is not against true expression of human emotion. Much abuse is done in God's name and by people pretending to be God, or Jesus, or the Holy Spirit. Survivors are therefore confused spiritually, mentally, physically, and emotionally and are mixed up about the "truth;" the truth of God's Word and the truth of what happened to them. DID is a spiritual problem, but not just a spiritual problem; it is also an all-encompassing life problem.

Most of the time, people who become DID become this way before the age of five or so. So for most, the core is an issue. There are many "protectors" who "come out" to protect in all different ways. Some protect by being quiet and submissive, some protect by arguing, some by fighting, some by sabotaging and causing confusion, some by crying and trying to gain sympathy, and many other possibilities.

The core must be protected at all costs because if the core dies, all die. As I stated before, this disorder is a disorder of perception. There are not really one hundred parts of a person, but it sure seems this way. Communication within can be done in different ways, but for me it was accomplished primarily through journaling. Journaling was the method that allowed me to write out all my feelings without fear of judgment. I protected that book carefully, though, and only let it be seen by my therapist. I literally kept it hidden from family members who could have been hurt by the words and pictures or like my former husband, hurt me with my own words. Yes, I drew pictures, too, and while I have never been an artist, the pictures were for my eyes and healing only. I did some collages of pictures from magazines. I learned some creative methods of getting my emotions out. I worked very hard for many years doing exactly what the therapist told me to do.

Communication was the factor that caused integration to occur. If my therapist told me to write about a certain thing, I wrote about it and did not return to his office until I had. If he told me to do "empty chair work," the thing I detest most about therapy, I did it to the best of my ability. I listened and hung on his every word. I wanted to be healed and whole and I wanted it bad. Inside myself, I developed a way to have all the parts communicate with one another and trust one another. I instinctively used visualization to "see" my parts through self-hypnosis. I sat with my eyes closed and concentrated on my thoughts of how my parts could communicate with one another. ART (Accelerated Resolution Therapy) is similar here. Though it is not hypnosis, visualization is quite effective.

There were many feelings connected to integration, some of which were loneliness because I did not hear "them" talking anymore. I experienced loneliness because I did not have anyone inside to talk to anymore, and surprisingly a decrease in functionality due to not being able to split to do certain jobs in the same way I had previously done them, nursing, for instance.

I am still a hospital R.N. I no longer do Medical/Surgical nursing. It is too physically challenging at this point in my life. I do psychiatric nursing and love that I show compassion to this segment of society that seems to be ridiculed by many. Contributing to this drop in functionality, as well, is that previously I could be focused on "just being a nurse." I did my "job" well, and when working, I was "nothing else but a nurse." I do not know if this makes sense, but this is how I experienced the process. Now when I work as a nurse, I have all my emotions to think about now; I am no longer a "nurse robot" perfectionist. I think about family things, God things, what happened on the news, the spiritual care of the person I am physically caring for, and many more things that take away from my "nursing focus." I do not think I am as good a nurse as I once was, but I am a much better human being. This is the most dramatic example I have for this phenomenon. I hope this does not deter anyone from wanting integration because my life did not truly begin until I became integrative. I am a well-rounded person now because I can do many things.

As a "multiple" (as we are called by each other and others that know us; it is not a derogatory term), we learn to do many different tasks to cope with life. Boy parts are more likely to want to camp, fish, and hunt, or work on cars, which benefits us later. In our female parts, we learn to cook, take care of a home and children, learn to nurture others, which benefits both male and female "multiples." We have very resourceful ways of learning what we need in life, though it may be different from the ways of others.

This poem explains some of my inner feelings both before and after healing integration.

Shattered Pieces Together Again

shattered pieces of china
are now together again
God provides the glue
I cannot comprehend

God is the Master Potter
He spins his wheel in time
when I come to Him
He starts making the china fine

His timing, His healing
my tears, my kneeling

together we work
I listen to Him
I hear His voice
I go where He sends

shaped by His hand
on the wheel I will go
formed by His love
why? He only knows.
His timing, His healing
my tears, my kneeling

why does He fashion this china?
I would not if it were me
but I thank my Lord, He knows best
what a merciful God is He

only He knows the purpose
of all clay He fashions in fire
to make fine china for His pleasure

is God's ultimate desire

His timing, His healing
your tears, your kneeling

This is a continuation and culmination of a poem written during the earlier times of my situation. It signifies how God healed me and can heal you. God has me "finish" my poetry this way a lot; it brings me much hope. What I mean by this is that I have written poems that are rather hopeless or not too happy, and finish them by turning them into a poem that displays healing.

I want to try to explain some phenomena that occurs in the person with DID. There is no safety in touch, due to shame about the abuse and much guilt. I had the feeling that I had no home and that I belonged nowhere. I believed no one wanted me because of what I heard as a child; this can vary from child to child. I remember not feeling "real," like I was a plastic figure or something, like being an inanimate object instead of a human being.

When I began therapy, I had many types of clothing and sometimes dressed like a girl, but not very often. I dressed like a man because I perceived that I was safer from male attack if I looked tougher. I dressed this ways for years and as I healed, I began to recover my feminine ways that included my clothes. Different parts dressed different ways. I do not know if my therapist could tell who was up front by my clothes or not. He told me that I gradually came to look more feminine, though.

I began to heal only after I began to have co-consciousness, which meant that my parts knew about the other parts. Gradually they were "introduced" to each other, some liked one another, and sometimes they fought amongst themselves. This was a very chaotic time when they were "getting to know each other inside of me." It was a critical time in my healing process though. When I wrote in my journal and visualized them coming together and we "talked amongst ourselves," then I could heal, but not before. This is the way I experienced integration. We never talked about anyone "being sent away," but always "coming together inside" to "live together in peace;" this method proved to be effective and healing.

Thank you for meeting my brave pilgrims. There are many protectors of the system. Then there are those whose job is to sabotage. I have learned to embrace and love them all. The more they have come to destroy, the more wounded they are I have found. This is a brief explanation of the internal system, certainly not an exhaustive one. The system kept me alive and well during my formative years. I will later explain my "safe place" that I developed while in therapy, which led to my healing, wholeness, and integration of my total self. I sure do thank all the pilgrims in my land, those who came to do their job and who did their job well. I am comforted knowing that each one of my brave pilgrims is now safe inside me and will forever be part of me, helping me along my journey of life. I consist of all of them. I can trust and love myself now. The brave ones were here seemingly on a short pilgrimage or sojourn; they were active on a relatively short-term basis in terms of my whole life span. Their care, their love, and their usefulness will be known and appreciated forever by the land of "I."

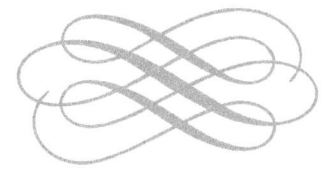

CHAPTER 5

MY SAFE PLACE

For God is not the author of confusion but of peace . . .
(1 Corinthians 14:33).

And let them make Me a sanctuary, that
I may dwell among them.
(Exodus 25:8).

Mind games were played against me. Narcissism played a factor in abuse. When people have been abused, they are victims of the mind games of their abusers; their thinking is mixed up. It takes time to recover proper thinking, through hearing the Bible taught and from working with counselors who will love them until they heal from the mind games played on them and reverse years of faulty thinking. This is what Scripture refers to as, "Be transformed by the renewing of your mind" (Romans 12:2), which refers to years of hearing right teaching of the Word of God. The thinking has to change about oneself and one's relationship to the world. It is cruel to call everything they have been through their own sin, for they were sinned against. It takes time to break cult programming. Some have even taught that the child who was abused sinned, though they were forced to do the act, sexual or otherwise. The child cannot be culpable for sin if they were forced on pain of death to do an act.

Pastoral counseling for discipleship is imperative for the person recovering from this form of coping in their life. Scripture has often been twisted and manipulated to serve the purposes of the abusers or is misunderstood in the person's mind due to confusion. Pastors or lay leaders must be willing to sit with people and give them the true bread from heaven. This was done for me in the early years of my treatment. I had 2 ½ years of biblical discipleship along with the first years of DID treatment. It was invaluable to my healing. There was Pastor Michael and a pastoral counselor, Sandra, who worked together and did this for me and a group of others.

I understand that even children raised in supposed Christian homes and churches have been affected by DID; it depends on the manner of abuse or trauma. Much depends on whether the Bible was taught with love and care, bringing God's love, instead of harsh, cruel judgment on the individual. For this reason, two aspects of healing, a trusted therapist and a compassionate pastoral counselor or pastor, provide a support system, especially if the person does not have family support. By support system, I mean a group of people who are healthy and committed to the person, ones who have time to invest, and ones who have the person's best interests at heart.

The support system should meet these criteria, whether or not it is a church or other group. The support system is vital to healing because no one can live in isolation. People need other people in their lives. I know some want to disagree with this statement, some quite strongly. I spent many years in total isolation from others because people were just not safe, but the isolation kept me bound in sickness. The only way out is to face fears, to do what we fear even though it is difficult. God created us all for relationship.

I do not currently know of any churches that are spending the time necessary with the DID-affected person to get them to healing; it takes years. I am sure there are some churches committed to the process; I just do not know of them. It can be a long process for a counselor. However, one can have church support without receiving all his or her therapy at that church. Pastoral counselors should be trained to handle these issues. It is enough for me to know that I can go to my pastor, ask him to pray for me occasionally and know he accepts me. I have told him briefly of my history and have his acceptance and care; this is enough. I have been healed, yet when I was in despair, this amount of interaction with my pastor would not have been adequate. Moreover, I do not intend to spend the rest of my life talking about this "stuff" or dwelling on the past. For me, I had to talk about this "stuff" with a pastor in order to believe that God did not reject me for it. The church of Jesus Christ should be reaching out to hurting people and helping them find the help they need. I got my initial help of therapy through the church I was attending back in 1997. It was through their referral that the therapy association evaluated me and the diagnosis was made.

I came to know that Jesus lived to die on the cross for my sins. He died on the cross because He was obeying His Father's will. God the Father wanted us to be in heaven with Him and the only way that He could accomplish that was to have His Son pay for our sins. Sin is not compatible with heaven so He had to deal with it once for all so that we could be with Him. I had the belief for years that God would forgive others, but not me because my sins were too heinous. I had a warped view of God, His Word, and His will. I did not know God in His character for years. Now I know of "His compassions they fail not, they are new every morning," (Lamentations 3:22-23), that "He is good! For His mercy endures forever," (Psalm 136:1), and that "Mercy triumphs over judgment" (James 2:13). Now, "I know that my Redeemer lives . . . ," (Job 19:25), and that "whoever calls on the name of the Lord shall be saved" (Romans 10:13).

A pastoral counselor, Sandra at that church, spent a few years befriending me. She did counsel with me, letting me talk about these issues. She prayed over me with many prayers. I am thankful for her input into my life. I believe her intentions toward me were good, though she was just learning about the DID issue. She has gone on to help many others. I have gone on to a different church now, but will always be grateful for her willingness to help me. She spent countless hours counseling me and I paid her in Mexican food! We laughed about this and had a great time eating lunch together at our favorite Mexican restaurant. Those memories are great ones.

When a therapist listens intently and thoughtfully to the patient talk about their memories, their fears, their pain of being betrayed by close family members or others who were supposed to protect them, and of their own self-doubt, trust can be built. It takes time to build trust and this is different for every person, according to the age of the person when the perpetration occurred, the type of perpetration, the personality of the person, and a number of other reasons. Self-doubt gets in the way of judgment. There is much self-doubt because the person has the feeling, so many times, that they are crazy, because "How could anyone really do this to a child?" or "How could my parent really do this to me?" or "I really am just crazy; these kinds of things don't really happen!"

Previous blocked out memories had to return to me and be fully remembered, relived even, felt, experienced with sights, sounds, and smells in order to be believable to myself, for me to own the memories. Only in experiencing them could I believe and validate myself that if I was truly reliving this, it was real because I could never make up this stuff. Before I remembered, I could not get past the feeling of being crazy, plus men I was married to and their family members called me crazy so that I began to believe it. Even with disorders, no one deserves to be called crazy. I realized that anyone faced with these memories would be in the same situation. DID is a somewhat normal reaction to very abnormal traumatic circumstances. Therefore, I could emerge from denial to face the intense pain, process the pain, and then move on.

The most important encouragement that I needed from my counselor when I began and then throughout my therapy was that he or she believe what I told them. I had two psychotherapists through these years, one for one year, and the other for twenty plus years. For a time, I got caught up in the questions of "Did these events really happen as I remembered them or were tricks played on me to make me believe they really happened." Trickery is a tool of the enemy Satan and is used often to create trauma by acting out rituals or murders or any other heinous crime to cause the child to "split," or to develop alternate parts, or personalities, as some called them. One of my therapists said to me, "I believe that you believe these memories; it does not matter if they really happened exactly as you remember them as real events or as tricks played on you. The impact is the same; they are real to you however they happened, that's what counts." This brought me comfort.

From childhood, I had the most vivid, terrifying, recurring nightmares, night horrors of the most evil kind. People murdered, tortured by myself and others, in historically cruel and unusual ways, as well as demons attacking, raping, murdering, destroying people—all were included in my repertoire of terrors. There were memories attached to each nightmare, each recurring throughout my lifetime, tormenting me until I fully faced the nightmare, the memory, remembered fully, and acknowledged it to my therapist "in the daylight."[37] When I had processed each nightmare in my waking hours, the fear involved never returned. There were so many, but they are now gone for good. However, this is how I can tell if another memory is coming, if I begin to have nightmares again. I have not had any new nightmare in many years.

There are many types of abuse: sexual, physical, verbal, emotional, and spiritual. The spiritual abuse is by far the abuse that caused the most pain in me, because of the confusion about God that it produced. Therefore, in therapy, it took months for me to begin to trust my therapist. I went through two other therapists before I found the correct match for me. In my case, it had to be a man. The other two were women; one was just not able to take what all I had to say about my abuse. I had a conflict with the other. It has always been more difficult for me to relate to other women. I did not trust other women back when my therapy began.

For many months during therapy, and perhaps longer, I really

---

[37] "In the daylight" is a term I use often, meaning "in the real world with another human being, bringing the exposed darkness to the Light and speaking it aloud."

wondered whether I wanted to be a Christian. I was not doing ministry at the time I doubted this, just working as a nurse. I would not have been able to be a Christian minister with those kinds of doubts in me, but they lasted a relatively short time span. Soon I realized the desire of my heart was to follow Jesus Christ. The reason I doubted was my family. I wanted so much to have my family's approval, fellowship, and love. I had to make a decision inside myself because I believe in heaven and hell. I had to say, "Whether I see any of my family in the afterlife, whether any are in heaven or not, I choose Jesus because I will see Him there and that is all I need!" I came to terms with my faith in this way, but it was so difficult. However, I hold the same opinion today and always will. It gives me hope in eternity, knowing that Jesus is there waiting for me and it gives me hope for a better life in this world today. I now have family members who are true Christians; I am very thankful to God for their salvation.

My safe place is my therapist's office. Every time I go in there, reeling and falling, I land in a safe place. For months in his office, I argued with myself, shouted at my abusers, and talked about my desire to be pagan. He allowed me to say everything I needed to say. I received a lot of healing the day that I screamed with all my force in his office, as I wrote about in my poem, "The Scream." I let out all the bitterness, frustration, anger and rage, resentment, pain, sorrow, guilt, shame, all the "bad stuff" I had held onto for so many years. He just sat there quietly while I screamed. Another staff member came in to see if he was all right. I guess it sounded as if I was attacking him or something. He just nodded at them that it was okay, and afterwards, I felt relieved. He trusted me not to hurt him; I'm not sure I could have anyway. I think this is one reason I feel so safe with him. I do not think I could overpower him physically, which makes me feel safe. I never want to hurt anyone else in my life and am more afraid of myself than of others.

When I needed my therapist to believe my memories, he believed them. He validated me. I knew that much of what I was saying aloud was almost unbelievable, even to me, so I questioned the memories. I knew that some events really happened and some were tricks to cause me to think things happened that really did not. I am not sure that he believed everything he heard me say, but what he did say to me was, "I believe that you believe everything you are telling me and it does not matter if it all happened the way you remember it now or not. There are parts inside who know what happened for sure, and in time they will reveal what was a trick and what was real, and the lies will come out." There was so much wisdom in his words and what he said is true. He saw me through when I had abreactions of abuse and neglect. I also am indebted to my therapist who cared enough about me to go to the hospital and shout at my inner parts not to hurt me, that they could not hurt me. This was when I tried to hang myself. They did not try afterwards. He was the one person who came to see me during my hospital stay.

My therapist's office is my "safe place to fall." I can say anything I need to say and do anything I need to do for my therapy. I can read my poems and papers to him, and he welcomes them all. He has time for me when I need it. I never have once felt rushed or hurried out of his office. He makes sure I have closure for whatever we are talking about before I leave. He makes certain I am in a "good place" before I leave his office. He allows questions, he allows me to carry the session sometimes if I need to, and he allows me to disagree with him, a real luxury. Authority figures never allowed disagreements in my experience as a child. I was bound by fear of anger and retaliation if I disagreed. I thank God for my therapist who gives new and superior rules in his office, rules to love myself and not talk bad about myself.

One of the goals of therapy is to comfort the person as they abreact to provide the comfort that the child never received during the times of abuse. The definition of abreact is "the expression and consequent release of a previously repressed emotion, achieved through reliving the   experience that caused it; the expression and emotional discharge of unconscious material (such as a repressed idea or emotion) by verbalization especially in the presence of a therapist".[38] Even as an adult, the child inside can receive the needed healing by the therapist as he or she gives comfort and expressions of care to them. I can remember thinking at one point how good God is to allow me to remain in a child state so He could have him there to provide comfort to that child. I had prayed a lot as a child, "God, why are they doing this to me? What did I do wrong? Why am I such a bad girl? Why don't they love me? I love them!" God answered this prayer, these many years later. I was not a bad girl. I did not deserve the treatment I received as a child. I do not know why they did those things and why they did not love me, but I know I am a lovable person. God loves me and that has to be enough, and is more than enough!

I had an experience that was very meaningful to me a few years ago, before my integration. I was in a restaurant waiting to get to a buffet table. Previously I had always said, "Oh, I'm sorry, I'll get out of your way!" and would wait until other people had gotten what they wanted first, even if I had been there first. I did this because of my severe guilt and shame. However, on that day, I stood right there, feeling as though I was on a mountaintop, and held firmly to my place in line. Now, what was significant about this seemingly insignificant experience was that, while standing my ground, while I never said a word publicly, inside I was silently screaming, "No! I no longer feel guilty for taking up space on the planet!" It was a real breakthrough for me. I did have a bad attitude toward people for a while after that, until that settled in me. I never again felt inferior to others or let others bring guilt or condemnation on me. I do not do that to others or myself anymore, either.

I never had the "luxury" of being on disability as I went through my therapy. I was tempted to go on disability; I had one caseworker willing to get me on government disability based on my emotional and mental difficulties. The people I was seeing in the public health clinic at one point were willing to say I was psychotic, but I would not

---

[38] Webster's Dictionary online. http://www.merriam-webster.com. Accessed 5/14/20.

allow that on my record just to receive help from the government. They said I had a psychotic break, a temporary condition when I tried to commit suicide. I heard a voice telling me to "hang!" I almost went through with the suicide. Afterwards, I filled out all the paperwork for the disability, and then changed my mind. In my heart, I knew I would be "done" if I had given in to that. For me, it would have been too easy to slide through life fading into the distance and felt I would never make a difference.

My family's values were such that it was wrong to accept government assistance, and these were my internal values, as well, so I would have been violating what I believed to be right. It was a difficult decision at the time. I could have easily received disability. My life could possibly have been easier in some ways, but overall I saw disability as a trap for me. It was worth it to me to keep my internal values while working and not rely on the government to take care of me. I feel much better about myself today.

Being on disability would have injured my self-esteem, and knowing what I know now, I can think more highly of my choices, having "fought through" the therapy, the pain, and even the physical injuries I received as a hospital nurse. The physical injuries were severe, causing me to need two spinal surgeries. I ignored my physical pain in lieu of my emotional pain many times. I did not take care of myself very well physically. I believe also that I was able to block out some of the physical pain, which did not stop me from continuing to injure myself. I often ignored my physical pain when I was working telling myself I had no other choice but to keep working. When I had pain, I used over-the-counter anti-inflammatory and muscle relaxant medications and continued to work. Maybe I could have chosen an easier route, but I did not know how to do that and maintain my self-respect.

Most of the years of therapy I had no insurance, which was detrimental to getting any medical care. I paid cash for therapy and that motivated me to keep working. After several years, my therapist agreed to see me pro bono and this was immensely helpful to me to continue therapy and on to integration. I lived for the day each week when I could go into the safe world of his therapy office.

Even today, when I enter the therapy office, it is my solace from the world. I can fully relax and find comfort. He has moved his office a few times, but it does not matter. Wherever his office is, is my safe zone. I continue to see him at intervals after twenty years because I want to ensure that I have learned all I need to know about living beyond DID. I am fully "in life" now and he is helping me to rebuild my life and avoid the pitfalls I fell into before. I fully trust him; he has never given me any reason to doubt him. He has never taken advantage of me or done anything abusive even when he certainly had the opportunity. He has taught me how to live again, how to love life, and how to love others.

Initially, I named this chapter "A Safe Place to Fall," rather than "A Safe Place to Land," because sometimes we have to "fall" on God's mercy and "fall" on other peoples' compassion so as to learn to trust. I addressed therapy first due to the nature of all that I went through regarding my spiritual confusion. It took seven years after I began to see my therapist before I was able to trust my current church. I had to know my own heart beyond any doubt before I would dare to become so involved in the Christian faith.

I was terrified that I would "poison" a church, as I stated before, and had to learn to trust God in me to know that my heart is entirely pure. However, I stayed on the fringes of my church for two years before I jumped in the water of fellowship. I say *jumped in the water* because it was truly a plunge. I first had to decide to trust myself and then had to decide to trust these people after all that had happened in my life in churches. After I went with church members to South America. I knew I had a home there at that church. I was able to use my nursing skills and the people showed care towards me.

My current church is not perfect, but it is perfect for me. It is all I ever thought a true church should really be, though I do not agree with everything that happens there. I have true friends there, a true pastor, and it is amazing to me. Finding this church was a long time coming in my life, but definitely worth the wait. It is definitely a safe place. I lived through a lot of bad situations in church before I found this one. I am involved in the music ministry at my church and am in a Sunday school group. I have many friends who have helped me through my most recent times of surgery, friends who have brought food, said prayers, sent cards, and paid visits to me. It is truly unbelievable to me what a true church can be like. I now have assurance of salvation. I struggled with this for years, believing that I was saved, due to words told to me as a child.

I am a worshipper of the true God. I sing and am very involved in church music, as I have been all my life. It makes sense that when the enemy comes against us it is through counterfeiting worship. Satan wants the worship that belongs only to God. Where we are gifted by God is where Satan the deceiver will attack us.

I met my husband at church; I remember the compassion in his eyes when I began attending there in our small Sunday school group. He saw me crying many times just in trying to stay in the Sunday school room. He saw me crying when I talked about my ex-husband dying. He was also there when I got ordained three years after I overcame all those terrifying issues of getting into church fellowship. I knew him for years before we began to date, though. We were friends first and it developed into the most loving, secure marriage relationship of my life. He accepts me as I am, with all my former wounds. He helps me daily. I was licensed and ordained at my church by Dr. Al Meredith (Brother Al). I received life-changing ministry and much healing here. I later became endorsed by my denomination.

I understand that there are parachurch ministries that do "Inner Healing," "Healing of Memories," and other types of ministries for the person with DID. I do believe that the person needs to come to a place of healing, and that most times if not all, remembering the memories is necessary.

Getting to healthier living is the goal. From my perspective, the work is just as difficult and it takes just as much time to learn new ways of coping with life past integration as it did prior to integration.

Whenever a person finds a ministry or therapist that helps them, it is well and good for them to reach out and receive their healing.

I have fully forgiven all the people who have hurt me. I do not understand what they were thinking and never will. Did those people think that all those children would just forget what had happened forever? I guess they had complete faith in their ability to cause us to dissociate and did not know that God Himself can take down any and every façade that ensnares the human heart. "To the only wise God, be glory forevermore through Jesus Christ! Amen" (Romans 16:27 ESV), and "For You are great, and do wondrous things. You alone are God (Psalm 86:10). The adults all delighted in playing God back in those days. They did not know the true God.

I did not forgive any of my family primarily for their sakes. It was only certain family members that hurt me, not all of them. I forgave for my own sake, for my own sanity first. It is also commanded by the Lord in His Word for us to forgive. When my mother apologized to me for not protecting me as a child, I forgave her right then and told her so. It was Grace that allowed me to extend forgiveness to her. However, I know that she does not know how to have a healthy relationship; she never learned. I forgive her repeatedly, but am very cautious about the time that I spend with her. The time is now very limited, as she lives with a family member about two thousand miles away from where I live. The arrangement has proven to be good for both of us. I am free and she is happy. We lived in close proximity most of my life. I was completely dependent and she was agreeable with that. She was controlling and my personality allowed that. I see her now two to three times per year and honor her as my Mother. I enjoy my time with her very much at this point in my life.

One mistake that people make is to think that if you forgive someone, you must stay in fellowship with that person, allowing them to harm you in the same way as they harmed you before. This is a mistake, because though they did that to you, if they have not truly repented, it may happen again. We never know if they have truly repented. I am not saying one must always break fellowship; I just want people to leave it open as a possibility for self-protection. One vital aspect of healing is self-protection; we must protect ourselves, which is a learned process. I said protect "ourselves" intentionally. It is our baby "selves" and child "selves" that were so wounded. Our inner world must understand that the adult "you" is strong enough to protect them now. Only then will they be willing to join with the core host to achieve full integration.

When people hurt me today, I try to readily forgive. Recently I had a new family member hurt me deeply, very deeply. It took me about three days, but I forgave because I knew it would make me ill not to forgive. Unforgiveness is poison to the person with DID. Sanity is lost, therapy progress is hindered, and health is impaired, not only mentally but also physically, by unforgiveness in a person's heart. Bitterness sets in and we become sick. It is a proven medical fact that many illnesses are caused by bitterness of soul and unforgiveness toward others. People living beyond DID cannot return to the place of unforgiveness and maintain their healing.

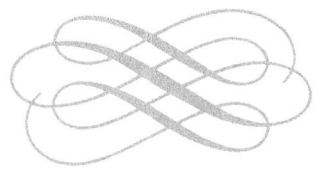

CHAPTER 6

MISSION JOURNEYS

*I beseech you therefore, brethren, by the mercies of
God, that you present your bodies a living sacrifice holy,
acceptable to God, which is your reasonable service.
(Romans 12:1).*

I have been blessed to have traveled to many countries for missionary
service short-term. Some long-term missionaries I have known
have said that these are unnecessary and maybe even harmful to
the people in the nations. I do not believe this as I have seen many
changes to people in the nations where I have been. These journeys
have also changed me time and again.

The first journey I went on was to Israel, which was several years
ago. I was part of the tambourine dance team and the prayer team
during this journey. We all had jobs to do and did them with all our
hearts. The team had approximately 30 people on it. We had pretty
dance dresses of white satin and sashes with sequins brightly colored.
During one of the dance times we were on the street in Jerusalem.
We were doing our dance routine and the leader said, "Stop now!
We have to go!" I did not know much at the time about following
authority figures and I argued asking, "Why? What's wrong? We're
not done!" One of the guys came up to me and put a sweater on me

covering my sequins. I thought they were crazy. What I did not know at the time was that we were being pursued by the police! I did not know that we were breaking the law, but the ones who reported us to the police told them we were proselytizing, which is against the law. We were dancing to Christian music of course. We left and got on the bus without incident. I learned to obey authority after this. Instant obedience is necessary when doing this type of work. Another time that we danced a guy came up to me and handed me a rose. I thought that was so cool. I had the best time dancing for the Lord. The Israel journey leader impacted my life very much.

I went back to Israel on a very different journey, a seminary journey. On that one we also went to Jordan where we met with men doing full-time missionary service. We walked and hiked all over Israel and Jordan backpacking through the desert. We stayed the night in a Bedouin tent with many other people. It was a reenactment kind of place. There were babies crying and dogs running through. It gave the feeling with sights and sounds of what it might have been like for the children of Israel to travel through the desert on their journey to the Promised Land from Egypt.

China was a fabulous journey with a fabulous leader from Bible College. We saw people saved in China, Vietnam and Cambodia. We worked with a medical mission in Cambodia where we ministered healing medicine at the jungle hospital. We saw a girl with typhoid fever on a straw mat getting an IV (intravenous fluids). We prayed for her. I stayed overnight in a hut with medical workers without my team. It was a special time where I was able to talk to two Cambodian girls who were working. They enjoyed practicing their English speaking. We did children's ministry, puppet and drama, Vacation Bible School and such. We went to a swimming pool where we did children's ministry and 120 children received the Lord. I have heard it said that it does not matter how many children make decisions for Christ, that those are not real conversions. I totally disagree. Children are very important people and should be respected by adults. The 4-14 Window of child evangelism meaning is that we should evangelize children between the ages of 4 and 14 to have the utmost influence for the Gospel on their young lives.

I went to China three times and had significant ministry times all three. I love that land particularly. On a seminary journey we went to the university in China and saw one particular girl get saved, one that I spoke with. It was the thrill of a lifetime; I left her in the hands of a good teacher to disciple her there.

On a seminary journey, we went to North Africa where we toured and studied. We were on a plane where we had to travel to another part of the country we were in. We had to leave under cover of darkness, which I found out later was because we might get shot down. We left without incident. There were so many times that I felt the Lord's protection on me and my team. I have gotten to know Jesus so much better on my journeys, stronger in my walk and trust in Him. I have healed more than I ever could have without going and the Lord knows what it took for me to heal of course. He also knew these would delight me and they sure have.

My team also went to Turkey studying the Bible and Paul's missionary journeys. I have been on twelve short-term trips with the Bible College and the seminary. It has been blessing upon blessing to my life to be able to go to these places and do the things I have done. Right now, I am in a time of "staying," which is something I never wanted to do. I wanted to be a full-time missionary, but I got married. I discovered that I wanted the stability of marriage like I always wanted in my life before my "missionary dreams" happened. I love being married to my sweet husband and who knows what may happen after retirement?

Going to the Amazon Basin was a great journey with my church. We went into the jungle and had previously unimaginable adventures. We trekked through the jungle, traveled down the Amazon in a very slow boat for seven days, getting off the boat to preach the Gospel to many who had never heard the Gospel. It was a dream that came true for me. Once, I was able to go on a speedboat down into the smaller tributaries with a small team of about six, just a handful of the entire group. Some did not want to go, but I begged to go.

We were able to interact with a tribe of people who welcomed us warmly. We played with the children and sang songs to them. We sang songs in Spanish that they could understand. The tribes living close to the Amazon speak Spanish, the trade language, while others living further away in the jungle speak tribal languages. We stayed close to the shore. I took pictures and showed the children the photos from my digital camera. All the people loved that. Next time, I would love to take a Polaroid camera and give them the pictures; it would mean so much to them. When we left, we escorted two children to the next village. The first child was a girl of about eight carrying a boy of about three who had typhoid fever. I could do nothing for him medically, which was entirely frustrating for me, but we had no supplies to give him. We prayed for the child; I pray he lived. They were precious children.

"There and back again" is about the best way I can describe the land that almost took my life. The Lord of the Rings trilogy is my favorite set of movies. I am a lover of cinematography and the lines in these movies actually helped me as I was traveling to this dark region of the world; darkness seems to permeate light there, but the opposite is actually true, though it is an intimidating land. I had memorized lines in the movie and those words gave me hope. There were many parallels with my travel to this land as in the trilogy. In my fantasy, I felt like Frodo Baggins. I learned that God loves this land very much because of all the people there. I also learned that, "He who is in you is greater than he who is in the world" (1 John 4:4). God in me was greater than all the darkness. I learned not to fear.

God loves people and sent Jesus Christ to die for all. In my heart, He sent me on a mission of love and compassion. I pray for that land today though I have not ventured back there – yet. Before I begin that story, I will tell of what led up to my having the privilege of traveling there.

Through a Bible College friend who I had gone on a previous mission trip with, I found information about the seminary. I had lived in the city of the seminary before and when living there several years past, I had driven onto the campus and prayed that God would please allow me to attend there if possible. I had and do have quite a burning desire to know God and know all I can about God. I did not know on the mission trip that the friend of mine was a student there; she is an international student. When she told me she attended there, my heart leapt. I cannot express in words the excitement I felt.

At my friend's nudging, I made an appointment to go check out the seminary. I was curious if I would be accepted and was, to my utter astonishment. I had had my doubts because my grades were low B's and C's in nursing school, but in Bible College I made A's and a few B's. They accepted me and I worked very hard to do my best. I took it very personally that I was doing the work to please God. I wanted my "Father" to be proud of me. I had a 3.8 GPA; funny thing is, though, I never thought I was intelligent enough to be a seminary student.

I proved myself wrong in that case because I did the work easily. God's grace was with me. Three years prior, God had given me the impression that I was to go to a very spiritually dark Eastern Asian country to take Christ's love to the people. I had been riding in my car doing ordinary things that day and singing to God with my worship tapes in my car, when I got the impression in a powerful way. I set out to find out how I could travel there, believing it was God's will for me. It seemed quite impossible because when I spoke to people in the Bible College about going, they told me, "You cannot go there. Only the most trusted career missionaries can go there." I know that God had led me to go there. I was determined to get there, to the Himalayan region, near Mount Everest, the highest mountain in the world.

When I began seminary, I went to the mission office and asked the director if he knew of any group that was planning to go to that land. He said, "Yes, as a matter of fact; in three months!" He knew of a very small team and put me in contact with the leader, telling me that if I was a good fit for the team perhaps I could join them. I met the leader, she liked me, I liked her, and I fit in nicely with the team. Only God could have set this up.

I attended meetings again like I had grown accustomed to doing.

It was an exciting time of preparation and prayer. First, we went to a large city near Mt. Everest. We spent about six days seeing various places in a neighboring country, visiting college students and friends of those journeying with me. The flight in-country was not bad, but we flew to the high elevation and landed at about 13,000 feet.

When we got off the plane, I immediately felt weak and dizzy. I did not faint then, but kept on going with the team. We rode a bus to the interior of a small city where the hotel was located. I was ecstatic to have finally arrived in the land that I just "knew" God had chosen for me to travel. Before we registered at the hotel, I sat on the front steps there because I was getting dizzy. After a couple of minutes, I fell over in a faint. I stayed "out" for several minutes and could hear what was said but could not respond. A couple of the team members carried me to the hotel room where I stayed for the next several hours. There in the room, I became violently ill with a sick headache, the worst headache I had ever had, and had projectile vomiting.

We had planned to do work with the street children in that land, too, and had prepared many puppets, games, and other fun things for the children for a "day away" of work for them and planned to buy their wares as we had been done previously in another country to compensate for their lost wages of the day. This was a different team; it was a good strategy again for the children to feel loved. This trip was different for me, as well, because we each were to handle our own monies, whereas a leader had always done this for us on my previous trips. I felt I was progressing in responsibility and abilities on the mission field.

I had been amazed at how God had changed lives of young college students through us in the large city and looked forward to working with these precious children of the land. It was not to be for me, though. After many hours of becoming sicker and sicker in the hotel room, my leader approached me to ask if she could take me to the local hospital. When I had first become sick, she had asked me and I had refused because I was terrified of being in the hospital in this primitive land. I was also afraid that if I were put in the hospital, I would be forced to leave the country. The second time she asked me, I agreed because I was very afraid at that point that I might die. I did not know what was wrong but knew that something "bad" was happening in my body.

The leader wisely brought me a can of oxygen that the local people had for sale and began to administer it to me, then got with me into a taxi. We went to the hospital. It was like no hospital I had ever seen before. It was a two-story building with long corridors. Some of the corridors had solid walls and some did not, some were open to the outside. In the emergency room, first the workers took me to the x-ray department where a chest x-ray was done. It was indeed a primitive set up, but real x-ray equipment. Then the workers took me back to the emergency room where my friends were. When I was wheeled back into a bed, a young woman was brought in, dead on arrival from a car crash. It was a bloody, terrifying sight.

The nurse put a real oxygen mask on me, saying that my oxygen level on arrival to the hospital was 65 percent. I had never been below 95 percent up to that time that I knew about. The normal oxygen level is 95-100%. I was gravely ill. Being a nurse, I realized how ill I was, so when the doctor came in and told me, "You have altitude sickness, cerebral edema, pulmonary edema, hypoxia, and need to be placed in the intensive care unit," I went willingly. He told us that I would be there getting treatments for three days and after that, I would be well enough to do usual travel activities. This gave me hope and I agreed, but not before gaining my friends' allegiance to stay with me the whole time I was hospitalized. I begged them not to leave me alone, and they did not, to their credit. They took care of me, loved me, and prayed for me.

My team members and friends brought food for me, emptied my bedpan, and helped me bathe when needed. I really was in the land that others had told me was impossible for me. I was sick, but I was there. It was an exciting time for me, though I was ill. My friends read the Bible to me, which gave me strength. I prayed that if God wanted to take my life while I was in that hospital, that I would turn it over to Him, and did turn it over to Him to decide. I had perfect peace. The Scripture became very real to me, which says, "Though He slay me, yet will I trust Him" (Job 13:15).

I was amazed at the nurses there, because though I was of a different religion than they were, they were very sensitive to my spiritual needs. They were sensitive to my every need, so very caring, and so good at nursing. The intensive care unit was, to my delight, the best unit of the hospital. It seemed like an ICU of about forty years ago that I had seen in photographs, but it got the job done. They had cardiac monitors and, thankfully, my heartbeat was strong and regular.

The medication I was given was Mannitol. In the USA, Decadron was the usual regimen for this problem of altitude sickness, but in this region, there was no Decadron available. The intravenous (IV) medications were very painful and "froze" my arm each time it infused; the sensation of cold was severe. Friends of my teammates had brought sheets they had from home, purple sheets. What a delight it was to sleep on these sheets from home, in my favorite color, no less. I was covered with a down comforter and was certainly warm. One of the friends gave me a blue pillowcase with white sheep on it; I treasure the pillowcase to this day. It is in my cedar chest with my most valuable belongings. It may sound silly to some reading this, but it was such a comfort, a little piece of home.

God gave me the grace to cope well with these treatments and to have a good attitude. I could never have endured the pain and discomfort, the fear and anxiety, or the terrors to come without the Lord Jesus Christ with me. I was quite afraid of death before that time and was afraid of seeing the dead in that land. The people of that land have very different burial practices than ours in the USA, very radical and cruel sounding to the average American. The name of the burial ritual is "sky burial." At a "sky burial," the tribal elders take the deceased person's body to a designated area and pound it with mallets. I am not sure what the instrument of destruction is, but the body is beaten down to nothing and the bones crushed. Whatever is left of the body after being beaten is left on the rocks for the birds to eat.

The "sky burial" is a sacred ritual to the people of the nearby Buddhist land. It terrified me to think of this, even knowing that I am an American and this would not have happened to me. It was in the back of my mind, though.

On the second night I spent in that hospital, a man was brought in to the bed beside me. I knew that this man was going to die and I told my friends so. I said quietly to them, "That man is going to die." They argued saying, "He looks okay to us," and they tried to reassure me that he was not going to die, that the doctors and nurses were taking good care of him as well as the other two of us in ICU at the time. I had "seen" it, though; in a vision. And it happened thirty minutes after the man was brought in, the tribal elders carried his dead body out of there, chanting their series of prayers, headed for the sky burial.

A bizarre thing happened after the death of this man. When they finished taking the man out, the nurses made sure their two patients, a young Asian woman and myself, had what we needed for bedtime and then turned off all the lights. We all went to sleep, nurses included! What a bizarre thing to have happen! I had been afraid of the dark up to that point, but after that I prayed and God gave me a peace about the dark I have never known before. Two of my friends were at the bedside and that helped. My fear of the dark is gone now.

God gave me an incredible gift while we were there. It was early June and the winter on the mountain had passed. Even in the summertime, though, as high as the mountain range is, snow still occurs sometimes. My bed was right beside the long picture window looking out over the Himalayan range. What a beautiful sight! It was simply breathtaking. I prayed that God would allow it to snow on the range so that I could see it when the sun rose, if I pleased Him. I asked Him for this as a gift of His favor if I was supposed to be there in the land. I told Him I wanted to see His magnificent beauty of creation. The lights were all turned out that night. I peeked out over the range when the sun was rising over them. Yes! Yes, it snowed! I squealed, cried, and felt so loved and cared for by my God, the God of all creation.

The team leader came to the hospital a short time later and looked sad. I had been praying that morning; God impressed upon my spirit that it was time to go home to America, that my time there had not been wasted, and that He was with me. When the leader came in that morning, she told me that her ministry leader authority back home said that I was to get out of that country – now. Her authority told her clearly that my life was in jeopardy and that he would not allow my death if it could be prevented. He knew that if I got into the airplane, that the altitude sickness would take care of itself. It was a bit sad, but when she told me this, I readily agreed. She had been praying that God himself would tell me this needed to be done and that I would accept it. God answered her prayers.

The nurses allowed me to get up to get dressed. It was the first time I had been allowed to go to the bathroom, as I had had to use a bedpan on the floor. I was in a land of eastern toilets, holes in the floor. I was surprised that I was actually able to use the bedpan on the floor; it became easier to use than a bedpan in bed, gravity and all. As I was dressing and looking out the window over the Himalayas gazing at the beauty of the mountains, God spoke to my spirit saying, "It is not time to die now." He was answering my previous prayer when I gave my life over to Him to take my life if He wanted. He answered not immediately when I prayed it, but at the opportune moment. I believed His words clearly spoken to my spirit that day. I believed He intended me to be "a living sacrifice" (Romans 12:1).

God gave me a new focus on life and I began at that point to desire to be married again. For the previous ten years, I had sworn off marriage for the rest of my life. I held onto the words I had heard inside myself, that it was not time to die. I worshipped God right there in that hospital room and sang to Him. Those words carried me through the entire trip home to the U.S.

My friends took care of me all the way home, too. My ministry leader rode with me on the long taxi ride to the airport over the mountains with an oxygen can in my hand and oxygen going the whole time. She told the taxi driver, much to his dismay that he could not smoke in the taxi with the oxygen going. He listened and drove faster than he would have ordinarily. I was not thinking clearly and would never have thought about that, even as a nurse. I was very ill, indeed. It was a fast and wild ride around the literal edge of the mountain, but we made it there. My leader dropped me off then went back to the team. It was up to me to get myself onto the plane, change planes in a major city, and then head back to the U.S. on a different airline. As I said, I could not think straight, so this challenged my mind to the maximum degree. Thankfully, in the first city still in the country, friends of my friends picked me up at the airport, let me get a hot bath, a pizza to eat, and a warm bed. They then put me in a taxi to the airport the next morning. I will always be grateful to those people, always.

On the way home to the U.S., the plane I was on had a bit of trouble. There was a storm some miles away and it affected our aircraft. The plane had strong turbulence and pitched violently. It was at least a 747, a huge aircraft, but soon the ceiling tiles began to fall. People were screaming and everyone thought the plane was going down. Even the flight attendants were screaming. I was traveling alone and did not care what people thought of me. I began to pray aloud in the charismatic way as I had done so many times at the Bible school. I prayed that God would have mercy on us and spare our plane. I remembered God said, "It is not time to die now," so I had a strong measure of peace that we would arrive safely, but I still prayed loudly. After I prayed, I went to sleep for about twelve hours on the flight, having perfect peace. The poor woman next to me seemed terrified of me when I woke up after a long sleep. She had been waiting to get up to the restroom until I woke up. I felt bad for her, but I had prayed in the way I did because I was afraid, after which God answered and gave me perfect peace to be able to sleep. God in His mercy spared our lives and we all arrived safely in the USA again.

God taught me many lessons on this trip to Asia and on the other trips I went on. First, He taught me that He loves me so much and that I belong to Him beyond any doubt, that He will always be with me wherever I venture to go. Second, He taught me that His enemy the devil is also my enemy and that that enemy hates me. Third, He taught me that the Word of God, the Bible, is truth, absolute truth. Fourth, He taught that He is always faithful and true. Fifth, He taught that the enemy has a bad plan for my life, but that He has a good plan for my life and for the life of every other believer (Jeremiah 29:11). Sixth, I learned that my life is not over yet and that He has an amazing plan for me, which includes marriage and travel with my hubby.

God goes to great lengths to teach me lessons. Perhaps this is because I would not listen any other way; I am not sure. I have been in situations of great extremes, and during and afterward, I have listened to God. He knows every child of His very well, better than we can ever know ourselves. I have been in deadly peril several times, but God has always delivered me. One thing is certain; I have never intentionally put myself in harm's way as a "death wish" or any such thing as part of a mission. God knows my heart and takes care of me; He is faithful. He taught me these verses from the Bible: "Blessed be the God and Father of our Lord Jesus Christ, who according to His abundant mercy has begotten us again to a living hope through the resurrection of Jesus Christ from the dead, to an inheritance incorruptible and undefiled and that does not fade away reserved in heaven for you, who are kept by the power of God through faith for salvation . . ." (1 Peter 1:3-5). He gave me assurance of salvation and of His love.

Sometimes, as a Christian, we do things that are risky because the multitudes need the Lord. Some people would disagree with what I did, but I believed the Lord led me to this ministry at the time. In some Asian countries, propaganda is placed on the street or dropped out of airplanes or helicopters. I was involved in a similar campaign though not from an airplane. This is how people there are notified of important current events. So, people pay attention to what is on the street around their homes. It was a risk, going out at night to deliver under cover of darkness. At one point, we were stopped and interrogated by police. They talked to us and told us we had to leave the city on the first bus out in the morning at first light. We did leave when told. We were not there to argue or proselytize, just pass on some information, crumbs of the Gospel. It was an exciting time years ago; I will never forget it.

I go as often as I can now to minister the Gospel to those who have never heard. Some people have heard, some have not. It really amazes me when those who have never heard before come to Jesus, as they did in Peru in a jungle village. In one Middle Eastern country, I was blessed to see a woman come to Jesus who was unhappy in her religion (not Christian). She wanted to follow Jesus but did not know how to start. She was dying in the hospital and weighed a mere 66 pounds. We gave her the good news of the Gospel and she gloriously received Jesus. She then told us she wanted to sing for us. She sang a beautiful song that she put on YouTube on her phone. The song was like the seal of her faith. It was so awesome! We were told she left the hospital a couple of days later, and a couple of days after that passed away at home. Now we know that she is with Jesus. God has blessed me to see many saved by Jesus Christ in many lands. I could not ask for more.

For me, following Christ has never been dull or boring. He has graced me to go on many international mission trips on five continents. I follow Him and do His work every chance that I get. I feel like a princess in all the things He has allowed me to do and all the places He has allowed me to go. I even love the element of danger that has accompanied me along my journey in following Him.

C.S. Lewis and J.R.R. Tolkien have affected my life greatly through their writings. One movie that influenced me in recent years has been Lewis' *The Lion, The Witch and The Wardrobe*. In this movie, I recall a line that is pertinent for this chapter, which is said about Aslan the lion, the Christ-figure of the movie. Concerning Aslan, it was said by Mr. Beaver, "Aslan is a lion, the Lion, the great Lion . . . if there's anyone who can appear before Aslan without their knees knocking, they're either braver than most or else just silly." "Then he isn't safe?" said Lucy. "Safe?" said Mr. Beaver. "Don't you hear what Mrs. Beaver tells you? Who said anything about safe? 'Course he isn't safe. But he's good. He's the King, I tell you."[39] This is just how I feel about Christ. He is always good and while He may not always be "safe" in this life, He is indeed "safe" when it comes to our eternal destiny; we can trust our soul to Him.

---

[39] C.S. Lewis, *The Chronicles of Narnia: The Lion, the Witch and the Wardrobe* (New York: Harper/Collins Publishers, 1978), 80-81.

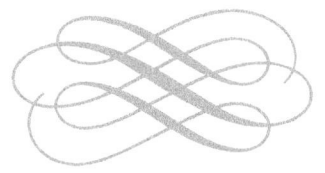

CHAPTER 7

HOSPITAL TRAUMAS

I was sick and you visited me.
(Matthew 25:36).

But to you who fear My name The Sun of Righteousness shall arise with healing in His wings; And you shall go out and grow . . .
(Malachi 4:2).

The work of recovering from DID is very intense and does not let up for quite a long time. The reason I am a Christian is that I believe Jesus Christ saved me for eternity, but also because of the strength that I believe He gave me for this work of therapy and survival in the here and now. I am thankful that God allowed me to go to nursing school when I was so young. I began at the age of twenty and finished at the age of twenty-three. I had seven stable years in nursing work before the memories and all the life trouble began.

After that time, I had many temporary jobs and a resume shows years of work history which I do not even remember. In spite of my being unable to keep a steady job, I always found work somewhere as a nurse. I was a single woman with no one who could support me during therapy. My mother was there for emergencies financially and for this I am very thankful. I appreciate her more than I can say. This took me a long way down the road. She would not allow me to live off of her, but she helped me at times. I did work full-time the entire time, not in one steady place, in many places, but always full-time. I worked full-time for a full twenty-five years since I became an RN. I guess my functionality kept me going in every way. It supported me physically with basic needs. It gave me a reason to get up and move each day though I hated it at the time. Life would have been so much easier to get up and think of nothing but the work of therapy. Often I resented that I had to work while friends of mine did not while going through their therapy. I cannot argue with the results I have obtained through keeping life going, however, as I am living a productive life still.

I was safe in my practice as a nurse. I was able to concentrate on my work while at the hospital. I was more careful than I would have been if DID had not been affecting me. I was keen on doing no harm to anyone. One of the beauties of DID is that it allows us to function well, at least for a time in adult life. I can truthfully say that no patient was adversely affected by my DID condition. When I worked as a nurse, I was "only a nurse." There were no other "parts" out to interfere. This means that I did not allow myself to do anything but completely focus on my work in the hospital and people got good care. I absolutely knew what I was doing when I was at work.

The reason I could not stay in a position for a long time was my absenteeism. There were days when I knew I could function as a nurse and other days I simply could not and knew it. I took many "sick days" off from work (these were really "mental health days," but I did not say this to my employers) and this inconsistency made nursing managers impatient with me. I do not blame them for their anger. I simply could not explain my situation. I protected myself from anyone at my job knowing about my disorders. I only told one nurse manager who was quite kind to me. I am not sure she believed all that I told her, but she was very kind. She told me I was an excellent nurse when I was there. She was an older nurse and retired a very short time after I left that position. I know she was frustrated with me, but she did not fire me. I am so thankful to her for that. I told her of my condition, and she was compassionate towards me.

Please understand, I realize that there are persons out in the world who cannot function like this. I do not want anyone to feel that I am judging if someone cannot do work and therapy the same way I did. We are all different persons and at all different points of functionality. If someone cannot function and work during therapy, then they cannot, simple as that. In no way do I intend to bring condemnation to anyone. I know there was a purpose that caused me to have a good means of supporting myself. No matter your situation, though, I am asking you to fight. Fight your way through therapy to healing. Do whatever it takes to get well, please!

In my work as a hospital nurse, I began to have occurrences that led to my having short flashbacks of memory. When I began to have flashbacks at work it really impaired my ability to work steadily. Flashbacks began to happen more as I developed more co-consciousness, which is the communication and awareness between parts. When everything began to come together, it took new coping mechanisms to combat the work difficulties. I would take a break with my journal many times, sometimes going in the bathroom for several minutes alone when it was necessary to write. I really thought I was losing my mind at first and did not want to go into those memories at work. I believe I thought if I could somehow get rid of nursing, I could stop whatever was happening inside me. Of course, that could not be, but I had high expectations of a new and better life other than working as a nurse, somehow, someway, after my rebirth as a Christian.

The desperation I felt led up to my surrender to God in my life. Nothing in life had worked out the way I had planned; it certainly did not turn out my way, and my life was not working. Here are some incidences of memories that began to come up in my circumstances that give examples of how this could happen.

The very first nursing job was working a busy medical oncology unit. I gave many doses of chemotherapy and did many things that I was unsure of because I was told it was required. I was so afraid that I would hurt or kill someone. I was not a cocky, new, know-it-all nurse. I was a terrified new nurse who lacked self-confidence. This worked to my advantage in the long run and to the advantage of my patients, for sure. When new nurses think that they know more than they know, they and their patients can get into big trouble. They learn very difficult lessons the hard way. The first nursing job was demanding and heart-wrenching to me.

At that time in the early 1980s, nurses did not have opportunities to be certified as we are today. I was not chemo certified then. I did the best I could and was very careful. As far as I know, I made no medication errors there. However, it was in this position that I learned how afraid I really was of death. I was afraid of dead people. I did not know why. I did not understand my childhood abuse at that time. After just a few months, I left that job and obtained another one in another hospital in the city where I lived.

The job at the new hospital was being a charge RN on an orthopedic unit on the three-to-eleven shift. The unit was a busy step-down trauma unit. We had all the trauma patients after they came out of intensive care. If the patient made it to our unit, they had a good chance of survival. I liked this job because people actually got well and went home, in most cases. People were not dying every day there and very few died while I attended there. I was only twenty-three years old and everyone else on my shift was in their late forties or above. I was the only RN and was the charge nurse. They, of course, resented having some "kid" telling them what to do. However, this is my favorite nursing job of my career. I grew very strong in my nursing role because I learned from all the older nurses and orderlies. I had a teachable spirit; I asked them questions and tried to learn from each one. They liked me after a short while. I did my best to be fair; I believe I was fair. I grew in confidence as a person knowing that I was succeeding on my job.

My life began to fall apart while I worked on this job, not because of my job, but because of my personal life. I was divorced from my first husband, married to my second husband, and then later separated from my second husband. I was on a bad roller coaster emotionally in my personal life. I worked on that job for seven years, and then decided I needed to move closer to some family in a large city in the same state. I lived near my sister and brother-in-law. I took my two sons to the new city leaving my job behind seeking new work and a start-over in life.

The new job was at a big city emergency department where there were always crises. I chose that at that time because I wanted to get the whole picture of the trauma patient from admittance to the hospital in the E.R, to the step-down unit, to going home well. I also wanted a big challenge.

I got the challenge of my life because I did not know my own limits, but I learned many new nursing techniques and skills in the process. I learned many things, bad and good, about teaching hospitals and medical interns and learned that I was still terrified of death. Strange things happened to me. I also acted strangely, I know. For instance, I worked the night shift, and they brought in a corpse that had partially decomposed. I never saw the body, but could smell the odor when walking by the door where they had the body. I froze in my steps, and could not move for several seconds, maybe minutes, as I am not sure how long I stood there.

The nursing shift manager was furious that the ambulance would bring in the corpse in that condition, knowing the person was long dead. No one noticed my reaction, as best as I could tell. I learned that I still feared death too much and had forgotten parts of my childhood memories and night terrors. The most terrifying was that I knew that I had people's lives in my hands and it was very difficult for me to cope with that knowledge. I did not want to be responsible for anyone's death due to my lack of understanding of my job. Again, I never had any mistakes on my job, but I was afraid.

My time there began to bring back these memories to the surface. I ran after seeing many disturbing sights, one of which was when a gunshot wound victim was brought in to the E.R. with a bullet in his heart, screaming in pain. The trauma medical team "cracked his chest" with no anesthesia, which mean that they punch a hole in the chest near the ribs then break the ribs with a separator to expose the heart. They said that if they gave him anesthesia, it could kill him. Therefore, they opened his chest that way, and then a doctor jumped on the gurney doing open heart massage on the man all the way to surgery. I do not know if he lived through surgery or not.

On Halloween night that year, there were many stabbings and shootings, as there are in any large city emergency department. There are certain days of the year, particularly some holidays that are more active with these kinds of emergencies. I remember that year, there were so many people brought in with shootings and stabbings that, when we checked them out, they were dead on arrival, and so many more waiting in line in the hall, some dead, some not. The ones who were beyond help, we tagged and rolled the gurney into a makeshift morgue. After we completed taking care of those in the hall, we had to go back and prepare those bodies for the morgue or funeral home. I noticed one of the bodies was tagged with the wrong name and a funeral home worker was wheeling them out to the wrong funeral home. We would have been in so much trouble. Thankfully, I caught the error and prevented a tragedy.

Another incident worth mentioning is that I got violently ill one night at work. My chest was hurting; I thought I was having a heart attack. One of the doctors gave me the "cocktail" that has three medications in it that, when taken, stops the pain if the diagnosis is ulcer or some stomach difficulty. They gave the medication to me and it showed a stomach problem, not my heart. They wanted to put me in the hospital to run tests. An hour later, I got a personal emergency call telling me that my dad had had a stroke in the town where he lived, about four hours away. I refused to go in the hospital and went to be with my mom and dad. I told them about my stomach incident, but it seemed so unimportant at the time. Dad had a stroke but lived and did well with therapy. After I knew he was stabilized, I went back to my job at the E.R. for a while longer ignoring my stomach problem. Others always came before me.

At that hospital, I saw so many tragedies, so much more than I could handle. The incident that made me go into a dissociative fugue state was when we were caring for a man who was yellow with jaundice. I was trying to fix a large tube that went down into his stomach from his mouth. Pure blood was coming out and the nurse I was working with said to me, "Get that bag changed! He is bleeding more; change the bag!" Well, there was a lot of pressure on that tube and when I pulled on it, blood splattered all over my face, my clothes, and the floor. I froze. The nurse I was working with said, "Go wash your face!" He said it about three times. I could not move. He finally grabbed me, and put my face under the water and washed my eyes in the eye washing apparatus in the sink. I stood up as if in a trance and walked out of the E.R. without completing my shift. I do not even remember doing it. I drove to my sister's home, terrified, and stayed there in bed shaking.

A dissociative fugue state is when a trauma occurs to the dissociative person and they "switch" into another part. They do not usually have co-consciousness, which means they do not remember what they have done or who they are at that time. They usually go to the original home, their birthplace, if they can. I went to my sister's house where I was living at the time.

I totally abandoned my E.R. position and never went back to work. I began to have panic attacks and irrational fears of getting a terrible disease like AIDS and dying. The HIV virus was just coming to the forefront in the 1980s when this happened and many healthcare workers were fearful. I had been terrified due to the blood in my face, but this had to do with more than just my fear of getting hepatitis or HIV. I attended to people dying with AIDS in that E.R. It is a tragic terrifying death.

I did go back weeks later when the nursing manager of the E.R. called me to come in just to talk to her. She asked me why I just walked away. I told her, to the best of my recollection. There were no repercussions for me, as I was still in training in the E.R. at the time of the incident, though I had been there three months. I had been terrified to come off orientation. I saw so many tragic and horrible sights, so many inhumane sights. I could not remain there. As I stated, I did not remember any of what had happened to me as a child at that time, so I just felt crazy. The manager told me that it is just not meant for everyone to work in that environment. I was grateful to her.

I tried to work at two other emergency departments of smaller hospitals, thinking that perhaps I could do that work; I could not. There were burn patients at one of the other hospitals that really got to me. I resigned my position after the burned patients were brought in and I had taken care of them, even though I had done a lot of other good E.R. work. One of the burn patients, a young man, told me, "Just let me die! Please let me die!" I could not take that at all. I continued to care for him until he was transferred by helicopter to a major city burn unit a few hours away. I had a panic attack after I left work that day, which caused me to realize I needed to leave the E.R. work behind for good. This was the same thing that had happened to me as a small child in the military hospital; I heard men begging to die. I knew about it only vaguely at the time.

The memories are fuzzy in some places, as you can well imagine due to my young age of three or four at the time, but some things are unmistakable. These things affected my adult life in my nursing work. I always wondered why I seemed to migrate to nursing situations that mock these bad memories. I do not know why and my therapist has no answer for me.

I knew that these memories had tormented me through my years of nursing work. A very short time after I fully dealt with these memories, I entered the chaplain program. I went through one section of chaplain education first and knew that I was to do a full year of training. The directors accepted me into the program. Within the program, we were able to choose a part of the hospital to minister to patients in; one or two persons in the program were assigned to the medical areas of the hospital. One or two persons were assigned to the surgical areas of the hospital, with one being assigned to the intensive care units and one to the burn units. I stubbornly decided that I needed to get all this past dealt with during my time in my education. Therefore, I applied for the burn unit and was assigned there for the entire year. It was difficult, but I learned to cope with the unit. I saw that the medical care was much more compassionate in the controlled and advanced circumstances today, very unlike 50-plus years ago. Even though I did cope with the burn unit, there are patients I will never forget due to their horrific injuries.

I saw a lot as a hospital chaplain. I saw a lot of grieving people who needed help. I helped with all my heart, with all that I had, but with the Lord's help. I could not do it in my own strength and the people did not need me, but Jesus. Many babies from the NICU (Neonatal Intensive Care Unit) and Labor and Delivery passed away. It was so sad. We did baby naming ceremonies for babies that had died. This was in lieu of baptism as babies must be living to be baptized.

I remember one particular patient in the Burn Unit who was so burned that he was slowly bleeding out. The slow drip of blood is an imprint in my mind. It could not be held in his body, so it dripped beside the bed. I have friends who are firefighters. I cannot imagine the trauma they have experienced through the many years of rescuing people. I know that it was so difficult for me in the controlled environment of the hospital, I cannot imagine being outside. In the hospital, there were many deaths, many grieving families, many terrified and tormented people, and many hungry people – hungry for food yes, but also hungry for a touch from God.

As a nurse, I never wanted to see an autopsy. As a hospital chaplain, I routinely have to do "morgue duty," which means that we are responsible for the bodies in the morgue, how many are there, where they are sent, and that they are sent to their proper disposition. We have to do a morgue census ensuring these details. This was just as difficult as the burn units to get used to. I wonder sometimes, why am I doing this (working as a chaplain in this hospital where such bad things happen)? Do I have to do this? Am I being self-punishing in doing this work?

For instance, I have had PTSD reactions in seeing bodies in the body bags after the autopsy, and sometimes just seeing them in the bag is enough. Sometimes just seeing the bags is enough to produce a reaction in me. I have seen some very difficult circumstances involving the morgue. The room where the autopsies are performed is just on the other side of a partition from where our morgue log is located. One day not long ago on a Saturday when not too many people were around, I was quietly writing on the morgue log. I knew there were people in the next room, but was not paying much attention. Then, I heard the sound of the autopsy bone saw, causing me to freeze in place. I could not move; I had a serious PTSD reaction and I was "back in that military hospital as a small child." It really took me aback. After I had counted all the bodies and finished my census as quickly as possible, I returned to the office and just sat there shaking for quite a little while.

I have five years' experience as a chaplain and loved the work despite the difficulties. I have worked in every area of the hospital as a chaplain and have done "morgue duty" on a weekly basis when there. I still go through my PTSD reactions at times. I do not know if I was being abusive to myself to stay in the hospital environment, but for some reason I believe I had to "conquer" these memories by confronting them in my adult life. I have done that many times with other jobs, gone back to "conquer" what I did not deal well with previously. It has been a pattern. I loved the diverse population of this county hospital.

As a chaplain at a Level I trauma facility, we must be present at all the Level I traumas in the E.R. So, I am right back in the situations that caused me unspeakable stress as a child, but now I am coping with these emergencies. There is some catharsis in this for me. Every time I go into a trauma area as a chaplain, I pray, thanking God that I do not have to work there as a nurse, being responsible if people live or die. I do not want that responsibility.

For about 3 years, I worked as an RN Sonographer. While doing this work, I had many wonderful experiences as well as difficult ones. Of the great memories, there were literally hundreds of women who said they were keeping their babies after they saw the baby on ultrasound. This was exhilarating to me. There were also hard times when the mother was determined to have an abortion even with seeing her baby. Also, hard times came when the parents were crushed when the baby was no longer alive in the womb. Sonography is very emotional, but so rewarding.

Another way I have attempted to conquer the memories is to do disaster chaplain work. I have not been to very many disasters at this point due to work obligations. I do not know what the future holds for me in this, but I am willing to be used by God. I will follow God's leading for my life. I am now in a good place in life where I can make informed and rational decisions about my future and am "in process." I may always be "in process." I would not be at all surprised.

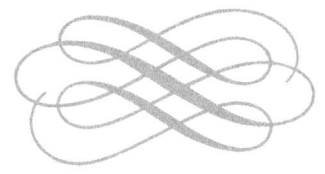

CHAPTER 8

LATER POETRY

But you are a chosen generation, a royal priesthood, a holy nation, His own special people, that you may proclaim the praises of Him who called you out of darkness into His marvelous light, who once were not a people but are now the people of God, who had not obtained mercy but now have obtained mercy. (1 Peter 2:9-10).

These poems are very deeply a part of me. In writing most of these poems, I have opened my inner emotions when it comes to healthcare in hospitals. Some caregivers might be able to relate from other specialties in healthcare systems. Allow me first to share two fun poems that I wrote during my chaplain education time. These two poems taught me to write not only when my inner being, the very core of my being, was troubled and overwhelmed, but during times of happiness and lightheartedness as well. In them, I write of very specific incidents that brought smiles to my clinical group and me. These are poems of celebration.

Evaluations

we made it, one down and three to go!
still alive and kicking
with "the storm" approaching soon
are we all still "sticking"?

wonderful day, food, fellowship and fun
Pat's great cooking, Leo's laughter, and Linda's funny tales
beautiful patio, nice cool breeze
encouragement, new "wind for our sails."

another work break, how great!
oh no! kitty licked the flan!
curled up little "innocent" Buttercup bathing in the sun
full belly, see that kitty yawn!

gentle tune of swaying chimes and birdies fill the air
peace and grace abound
quiet ripples of the rushing water
ripples like music make a lovely sound.

sight of gorgeous flowers in the garden
like angels with their beauty
such a lovely day to be outside
filled with fun yet duty
because of your comments and camaraderie
I eagerly anticipate the next time of fun
I enjoy being your fellow traveler
thank you everyone!

The kitty licked the flan that one of the teammate's wives had prepared for us. It was just a small lick and as I recall, that part was cut away and we enjoyed the wonderful taste of the rest of that wonderful Mexican dessert! The supervisor, Leo and his wife Pat, have a beautiful little quaint home with a beautiful patio and many beautiful flowers, several birds in their cages, and two or three cats. It was such a fun time. It made a work evaluation bearable and enjoyable, even. This evaluation was after the first three months of the work at the hospital. I believe the Lord was preparing me for the hard days of work ahead where I was forced to look inwardly at myself with the purpose of learning to minister better to others. I returned to this wonderful memory many times over.

Reflections on Our "Group Process"

it is the honeymoon!
when all is well and no one speaks their mind
with lots of love and acceptance
everyone says, "we're just fine!"

three months of wedded bliss
for five people all together
for that many people trying to get along
there has to be stormy weather

is this a marriage? no surely not
but it is a work of reconciliation
between God and man and man and God
why then must we have confrontation?

when I say "man" I mean humankind
woman and man the same
all created in God's image
as stated by the Name
the Name is of the Triune God
as introduced in Genesis
whose family we now belong

if we believe in Jesus

He is our Hope of "wedded bliss"
in eternity we'll honeymoon
then we will rise above the storm
and will be fine like a wedding in June

The following poems tell my deepest heart's cries of the time of
my hospital ministering process.

Desperate for God and Called

Will you love these people?
can you, will you love
the victim and the perpetrator
the abused and the abuser
the helpless and the hateful
the babies and the parents who put them
in harm's way
the rich and the famous as
well as the downtrodden on the street
the hungry and the satiated
the knife and gun club and
the innocent ones far from home
the unlovely as well as the lovely
the untouchables as well as the beautiful
the ones from distant shores
the ones who will never believe as you do
the ones who will not listen to reason
the tired and the needy and sick
the wounded and lame and maimed
the ones who will not love you back
the rude and the crude

the haters of people and haters of God
the prisoner and the guard
the police and the arrested
the prostitute and the pimp
the shooter and the shot
the rapist and the raped
Who am I to minister to these?
I am unworthy but willing
I will love them but not without You Jesus
I cannot without Your Grace
I will follow where You lead
I will speak as You give me the words
I will believe and care
I will trust in You.

The responsibility and trauma was beginning to affect me deeply
and my poetry reflected this difficult yet necessary change.

Sometimes

sometimes I feel blessed
sometimes I feel cursed
sometimes I feel weary
sometimes I feel confused
sometimes I feel unworthy
sometimes I feel energized
sometimes I feel jubilant
sometimes I feel miserable
sometimes I feel incensed
sometimes I feel used
sometimes I feel calm
sometimes I feel out of control
sometimes I feel resilient

sometimes I feel overrun
sometimes I feel mad and sad and glad and bad
all in the same hour
mostly I feel desperate for You, O my Lord!

❧ ❧

I thank God that He taught me that it is not all about me; it has very little to do with me. I am there to minister to many people, as many as possible. In order to do this, however, each of us must deal with his or her own "stuff," his or her own past history, his or her own "story," his or her own emotions.

Each poem represents someone or a group of persons that I have cared for at the county hospital and some in remembrance of other hospitals where I was a nurse. I have cared for many and to make my position very clear to the reader, my faith is such that I believe I need God for every interaction that I have with every patient. I believe that I need God's supernatural strength and energy to minister. Some chaplains, pastors, and others in ministry believe that they can minister in their own power and strength from their acquired knowledge. I am not complaining about those ministers because I understand that God gives us grace to do everything that we do as individuals. He leads us and as long as we walk with Him, He will guide and direct. It is just that in these extreme cases, I find myself praying and crying out to God very often, very often. If I get afraid, I pray. If I get shocked or surprised, I pray. I believe in the power of God to answer my prayers and lead me on.

Will You?

Will you …
take care of the gunshot victim in one bay
and the shooter in the next
what about the one burned while he lay sleeping
in his own bed, in one bay and the drunk person

who burned him with carelessness in the next
what about the abused child lying burned in her burn unit crib
and the mother who burned her on the cot next to her
what about the man cursing God because
his whole family turned on him and
the ones he raised with tender loving care as his own
tried to beat him to death
what about the parents hating children and the children
hating parents
what about the mentally ill who speak God's name in prayer
in one breath and curse Him in the next
such paradox in this place!
Will you ... take the time
will you love them all
"O God I cannot!" I exclaimed
Will you?
"Grace! I need Grace! I cry out
Grace is His answer.
"Lord by Your Grace alone can I,
because of Your great love and mercy will I." Amen.

That One

Can you care for that one?
which one, Lord?

the one who cheated and lied
the one in desperate straits
the one who murdered friends
the one cursing you with vehement hate

the one who cut
the one who bled

the one who shot
the one found dead

the one bringing temptation
the one in pain
the one who used
the other for gain

the one who lives
on the dark side of life
the one who tried
to kill his wife

the working poor
the mom and dad
who tried to feed children
but spent all they had

the addicted, the convicted
the ones bound by drugs
the one who protects
and cares and loves

the poor raped child
who hurts so bad
the helpless mother
the rapist dad

the burned-out nurses
the tired and poor
those weary of caring
and trying to endure

the caregivers who see
so many horrible sights

who toil on the holidays
weekends and nights

the doctor and nurse
who cannot give more
their health and their sanity \
God can restore

so many to care for
with so few resources
the never-ending battle
of spiritual forces

yes I will care for
each one that I can
but I do need Your help God
I am nothing but "man"

with Your help and Your care
and Your mercy and love
I can care for these precious ones
You love from above

which one, that one
the one of Your choosing
the one who is winning
or trying or losing

to this work You have called me
with You let me walk
I need You so badly
I can't even talk

don't leave me alone Lord
only with Your help can I bear

when You and me are together
only then can I care

❧ ❧

These poems reflect my honest struggles with my own human
emotions in caring for others, caring beyond my human capabilities.
Here is another poem that I rewrote after all this hospital training
was completed, one which reflects more healing within.

No Train Wreck in My Soul

There is no more a train wreck in my soul
The Lord intervened and made me whole
He told me of His love and care
And said He will go with me everywhere
He is my loving Father true
And I said, "Lord, where You go I will follow You.
He said, "Come on child, come up higher,
And put away your thoughts of fire;
I will show you a better track
One you will go down and not look back
I will show you a better gate
One not covered with fear and hate
Because you are sad means that you are alive
Do not be ashamed because you thrived
Do not take on guilt others try to contrive
You are right in the center of My plan
One I intended for listening "man"
You hear My voice you hear Me true
And all your life I will be with you
And give you all the things you have missed
Forever My child seek My face to kiss
Keep looking up My child
You have not passed your day

You have not missed your ship
It is not floating away
I am your Captain and the Anchor of your soul
And you know what that means
Hope personified has made you whole!"

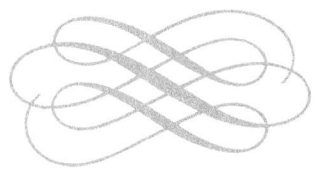

CHAPTER 9

ABBA'S HOUSE

*He [Jesus] brought me to the banqueting
house and his banner over me was love.
(Song of Solomon 2:4).
For you did not receive the spirit of bondage again
to fear, but you received the Spirit of adoption
by whom we cry out, 'Abba Father.'
(Romans 8:15).*

The Scriptures above have meant so much to me, particularly at night and during my journey to Abba's House. Scripture states, "For you did not receive the spirit of bondage again to fear, but you received the Spirit of adoption by whom we cry out, 'Abba Father'" (Romans 8:15). Abba means Father in Aramaic. I know now that I am adopted by God my Father and am "accepted in the Beloved" (Ephesians 1:6).

Envisioning Abba's House sealed my healing integration from DID. "Abba" is my favorite name for God. I always desired protection in my "Father's" house. I wrote the story of how my inner journey transpired.

The journey to His house at first was agonizing, grueling, and wearisome. It seemed such a long journey in the beginning. There were times I thought I never would find that home in the woods. All around me were dark woods full of dark shadows. It was scary to me in the dark woods. Nonetheless, I knew that the only way to proceed was to move deeper and deeper there.

I begin here with the poem I wrote about the journey while I was in the midst of it, before I reached my destination. The poem is written with a 1-4 rhyming sequence, which does not seem to rhyme at all and sounds oddly dissonant. It seems "out of sync," just like my life. I "march to a different drummer," as my first clinical nursing instructor informed me in 1979. She did not mean it as a compliment. My therapist told me more recently, when I read this to him that, "Yes you march to the beat of a different drum – God's drum!" That made me smile within my heart.

Later, I revised the poem, which was quite healing for me, healing in greater depth. Here is the first, dissonant poem:

I Took a Walk in a Lonely Wood

I took a walk in a lonely wood
With shadows creeping near
They sought to overtake me
When near the clearing I stood.

A shack? A barn? A hut?
What could that really be?
Are my eyes deceiving me?
And what is this aura, a hallucination, what?

The children gathered round
Each huddled by their own tree
Guarded, cringing, angry, lonely
Who dares to make a sound?

Each one a special child of God
Though believing none would dare

Except for one who holds out hope
Like a seed from a flower pod.

Together again though remembering not the core,
Life has been strangely separate,
Confusing, dismal, dark and heavy like those woods
Nevertheless lightened by the wondrous sight of a door.

Where can it lead? Whose can it be?
Is it dangerous, sinister like the fairy tales of long ago?
Or is it good? Who lives there – or what?
Are my eyes deceiving me or do they truly see?

Standing in a garden outside
I caught a glimpse of Someone
Should I approach, go back, go around?
So compelling as I approach – No! Go run and hide!

But so tired of wandering always so alone,
Cold and dark out here in these woods
Will I ever feel the warmth of love, touch, safety, and tender care?
So many wicked, dangerous seeds I've been told I've sown.

I have believed so many lies of decades of years gone by
So many roads I've traveled in so many differing directions
Don't I deserve a "bye"?
Relief from my many cries?

I wrote this as I looked back on this journey during my chaplain
training when I was looking so closely at my life, a difficult task for
me. I wrote this as a non-rhyming poem because it better symbolized
the perspective I had on my life at that point. This poem is about
my approach to the Shepherd's Hut, which later came to be known

to me as Abba's House. I had forgotten that I first noticed the blue door. I first envisioned the house as a "hut" such as from Cambodia, then later as a country home with good, warm, comfort food, and extreme peace. This is the way I see it today.

The story goes thus:

One day I was walking in a lonely wood of an old growth forest. There were trees planted closely together, not by human hands, for this was a wild wood. It was a dense forest, so dense it made walking in the darkness difficult. I could see where to step but the shadows were intrusive upon my emotions – I cried out inside myself for light. I hungered for the light. I wandered aimlessly for some time in this forest, not knowing where I was or where I was going.

Some of my "children" [inner parts of me] loved the darkness and all the trees that they could hide behind. Each chose to hide behind a special tree of his or her choosing. At one point, I was able to get a few of them together along a path and encouraged the ones who were braver to invite the "scary ones" to join us. The "scary ones" were not so scary to me at that point, but they tried hard and did scare me for many years. They did a lot of talking among themselves and with me; it was a good time of communication even through the discomfort of these dark woods. We journeyed on together, with many lagging behind but still moving forward. We had done much work in journaling, communicating with a lot of co-consciousness for about three years before this happened. On we went through the darkness. Many of the child parts were skeptical, as was I, but we knew we had to make this journey. We were soon delighted.

A faint light, a spot of light, in the distance surprised me. I crept closer, following that aura. Then curiosity took over and my pace quickened. It was a clearing! There appeared to be a small hut. I called it a hut because it was far away. As I approached, it appeared to grow in my perception. I was simply drawing closer. I could see it was a beautiful little country home, a cottage like an old English cottage, very beautiful to my eyes. In front of the home were beautiful flowers of every kind imaginable, flowering fruit trees with fruit on some of them, flowers on others. Such a contrast it was from the dark forest I had seen when I first wandered in. I hoped the children were following, but I got so excited I did not turn to find out.

A man stood near the front door and I wondered if he was someone who worked there as a gardener or if he was the owner. Still a distance away, it was difficult to tell. We stood at the edge of the clearing a good long time, then I saw the Man's eyes, full of Light. The Light shone with love, peace, grace, mercy, compassion, and comfort. I felt utterly compelled to go to Him.

At the time that I noticed His eyes, He stretched out His arms and I could see His beautiful white robe that glistened with every color of the rainbow: red, orange, yellow, green, blue, and purple. The colors glistened and twinkled. I was mesmerized. His arms invited me to come toward Him, closer and closer. He welcomed me at the door, welcomed me to His house, His home for me to share. I never felt so loved and welcomed before.

I called Him Abba and He said that pleased Him very much. He led me to see what was inside that beautiful cottage home of His. It was a delightful sight, a warm fire in the fireplace and soft, comfortable furniture covered in fleece. It was a very warm, toasty home and took the chill of the dark woods right out. We went into the kitchen where there was another fireplace for cooking. A pot in the fireplace with a wonderful stew on to cook was so inviting! On the kitchen table was a pretty tablecloth and many wonderful things to eat, such as piles of cornbread with butter, much fruit to eat, no doubt grown on the fruit trees outside, fruit such as I had never seen. The fruit was big and beautiful. There were many treats on the table, and a side table with all of my favorite foods ready for me to eat whatever I wanted. I knew I would never be hungry again in this house!

I felt completely loved and cared for. There was much light in the house, no dark corners. Abba lighted the house; what a wonderful sight. I felt so very warm. After I had eaten my fill, He wanted to show me the rest of the house. He showed me the door to the basement and

I cried out, "No! I cannot go down there!" Very calmly, He stood by me, holding me, and said to me, "You are in Abba's House. Nothing can hurt you here; I am here. Everything is lighted, even the basement. There is nothing dark here, as I know how afraid you have been of the dark, my child. I love you and nothing will hurt you while you are in this safe place. I believed Him; I took His hand and He led me downstairs. I was not at all afraid.

We walked down the stairs. There did not appear to be much down there, no furniture. It was warm and cozy down there, though, not like a dark, dank basement with evil things going on, as I had known before. I walked all around the basement not knowing what I was looking for until I saw a pink light coming from under the stairs. It was a bright and beautiful pink glowing light surrounding a baby swaddled in a beautiful, pink fleece blanket. The baby had chubby cheeks and looked happy. She was cooing and I knew she was "baby me." I picked her up and cuddled her in my arms, holding her close to me, loving her for the first time, ever. Abba said, "See, she has been safe with me all the time. I will keep you for all your life. You are mine and I am yours!" Abba oozed with love that was tangible when He spoke. I placed "baby me" down carefully in her little place, smiling. She smiled back and laughed with delight. I knew then she was my core.

"There is something more I want you to see before we leave this place." I was glad to keep looking. In a different area of the basement, I could see a haze of blue light. I wandered over in that direction and turned a small corner, and there I saw him. A bright and beautiful glowing blue light surrounded a baby boy who was swaddled in a blue fleece blanket. The baby boy cooed and laughed with delight right aloud when He saw Abba. Abba said to me, "See, this little boy is happy now, and safe with Me. He will never be hurt again. Unlike you, He will never grow up because he is the baby that you thought you killed back when the bad people were hurting you. But you did not kill him, they made you think you did. You did not. He did indeed die, but he is forever with Me; see, he is happy and I love him very much!" This was the baby boy in my nightmares and early memory of childhood.

I began to cry, to weep, to wail; Abba held me while I did. He did not try to hold back the tears or tell me I was wrong for crying. He just loved me as only a good Father would. I realized as He held me that all my parts were present and crying and He welcomed them all. He accepted us as we were. This is when we all felt safe enough to come together because we were all so drawn to His love, His irresistible love. We let out all the emotion of years, and years of guilt and shame until all the bloodguilt was gone. Abba clearly told me I did not kill that child. He told me that the child was with Him forever and could never be hurt again. I knew now that I was "one" (whole) and always would be; what a marvelous feeling to know that all of me accepted my Lord and Savior. Words cannot describe the emotion I felt.

Abba said that we should move on now and we went back upstairs. He told me he had some other rooms to show me on the way. On the way, I glanced into one of the bedrooms and there was the softest looking feather bed with a beautiful quilt. It looked so inviting. He told me I could rest there in just a little while, but He had something else to show me first. I went with Him outside the front door and was amazed at what I saw. I saw a big, larger-than-life wooden cross. When I saw it, I knelt and wept some more because I knew Abba's Son was Jesus who died on the cross for all my sins. I laid all my cares there at the foot of that cross and stayed there a good long time, talking with Him about my life.

Abba invited me to stay in His house anytime that I want, His beautiful country home. It is a haven of love and peace to me. I turned to look and smoke was curling out of the chimney at the top of the house. I knew it was Jesus' house and would be my house always, too. It is my safe place and always will be. It is a mansion to me, a simple country home with plenty of Love, plenty of Grace, lots of spiritual food, and lots of physical food to eat, as well. I never again have to worry where my next meal will come from. I will live there with my Abba both now and forevermore. "Thank You, Abba."

Abba said a few words that mean much to me. He shared how much He loves me and not only me, but all others in this world. He gave me the charge to go out from our House and minister to others, but come back here anytime I need or want to. He told me to invite others and bring weary travelers here. He told me also that He would lead other weary travelers here. He also gave me the charge that when I go out of the house to be sure that I leave the fire stoked in the fireplace to keep it burning so the good warmth will stay in the house, to leave fresh cooked food on the table, to make the beds, and be sure the babies are warm and kissed. He said there would be more babies in there as more travelers came. Writing this book is my way of leaving the fire stoked to keep the house warm, leaving fresh cooked food, making the beds, and making sure the babies are warm and kissed.

Abba said He would show the new travelers around if I brought them. He would bring others, as well, He said, and would do the same for them as He had done for me. I thanked Him and promised that I would do my very best to obey His words. He said, "I know you will, child; now go in peace and in the love of your Abba always!" He melts my heart. When I fall down, He takes my hand, lifts me up to Him, and looks at me with the love of the perfect Father and holds me close.

Since He led me to His house, I feel safe inside myself, all my parts are welcome, and each is free and safe to integrate and live together harmoniously because we all accept Jesus now. There were parts that did not want Jesus. Others wanted Him more than anything in the world. He drew them all to Himself and convinced them of His love for all of them unconditionally. I am now wholly Christian and live in the love of my Savior and Lord. I know my Abba loves me unconditionally here in His House; He saves and cares for all of me.

Welcome to my vision, which saved me and healed me by my Father's gift to me. This came to me as a vision within myself; it is a very real place to me inside my soul. Persons affected by DID have creative minds. I do not intend to exalt myself when I say this, but rather exalt the God who gave me a creative mind. I simply say that

God's gifts are real and true. Every single person alive has a spiritual gift; he or she must seek God to find it. Many people think they do not have any gifts, but this is simply not true. Circumstances have taken away our perspective at times, but we must never give up.

God makes a way out of every foul circumstance we can find ourselves in, in life. After a couple of years passed, I healed even more. I rewrote the poem about the approach to Abba's House, which reflects my life's journey.

I Took a Walk

I took a walk in a lonely wood
With shadows creeping near
As I happened upon a clearing, I stood
In trembling, craven fear.

A shack? A barn? A hut?
What could that really be?
Is that an aura, hallucination – what?
Are my eyes deceiving me?

The children are gathered all around
Under the shadow of their own tree
Guarded, cringing, none dare to make a sound
O, how I long for them all to be free.

Each one is a special child of God
Though they do not all believe
But Hope is as a bloom birthed from a flower pod
And Hope some do receive.

Now together again, though who is the original core?
Confusion within, heavy and black as coal
Nevertheless "lightened" by the sight of a door

The Door opened to the light that pierced the night of my weary dark-clad soul.

A door! Where does it go?
Where does it lead?
Is it dangerous as in fairy tales of long ago?
Or is it good – what do my eyes truly see?

I caught a glimpse of Someone
Standing in the garden outside
Should I approach, go back, be done
No! Go run and hide!

O so compelling I'm drawn to Him
I cannot help but go
He draws all the little ones close to
Him And from Him they refuse to go.

This Someone can be trusted
He told me Whose I am
He led me to the core; my life adjusted
And He leads me by His hand.

So tired of always wandering alone
In those woods so cold and dark
Will the warmth of a safe place ever be known?
And love, that gentle spark?

Many roads I traveled in decades of years gone by
And having believed so many lies
I wandered in so many different directions; don't I deserve to cry?
Believing lies, I was so unwise.

But Wisdom never gives up
Wisdom never recedes

Wisdom is only from God above
And He never gave up on me!

Hope provides my solace
From all those lonely years
Now all the children can laugh and play
And have joy instead of tears.

Hope was the key and Faith unlocked The Door [Jesus]
All the children are together now living completely free
The Door is wide open forevermore
And I never gave up on me!

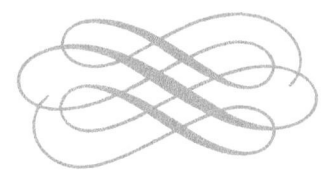

CHAPTER 10

BRAND NEW LIFE

Trust in the Lord and do good; dwell in the land and feed on His faithfulness.
(Psalm 37:3).

If anyone is in Christ, he is a new creation. The old has passed away, behold the new has come.
(2 Cor 5:17).

Hope happens. God has truly given me a new life and new love. My life is turned to health and wholeness; it is wonderful. My hopes and dreams turned out to be much different than I expected when I began Bible College. I found myself desiring stability, steadfastness, faithfulness, and even marriage. It became the desire of my heart after my hospitalization in the Himalayas to have a husband to serve God with and to be able to talk freely with about our relationship with the Lord Jesus Christ. I began to look around, but it took me about three years to allow God to open my heart to let someone else come in to share my life.

God gave me a Scripture about my future marriage relationship. I did not desire marriage until God put that desire back in me while in the hospital in East Asia. I had given up thinking I could "do marriage," and I just wanted to be a missionary full-time. God had other plans for me and for that I am very grateful to Him. The Scripture is as follows: "Do not fear, for you will not be ashamed; neither be disgraced, for you will not be put to shame; For you will forget the shame of your youth, and will not remember the reproach of your widowhood anymore. For your Maker is your Husband . . ." (Isaiah 54:4-5).

God reminded me that the original desire of my heart was to be married and raise children in a loving home. When I was a child, this was the extent of my ambition. There must have been something of God in this ambition; yes, He calls some to family life. I did not think about missionary service. I wanted to help people, but mostly I wanted to be a mother, a good one.

Widowhood is more than just having a husband die. To the women in biblical times, it meant poverty and possible starvation. It was a reproach. It remains a reproach in our time also. Many times widows' grown children ignore, abuse, and/or place their mothers in nursing homes and forget about them. This is a sin against their parent and against God. God has a lot to say about honoring parents. Even if it seems the parent is not worth honoring because of what they have done, we can do our best to honor them for giving us life. If this impedes the healing process, yes, other arrangements have to happen and fellowship is not necessary if it means one has to stay bound in their disorder. However, it is never right to abuse, neglect, or abandon a parent. We can be sure they get good physical care and make our contact with them minimal, one option.

Reproach can be the same in marital abuse and divorce. Women usually have lower incomes after divorce. Women are usually reproached by society for being a divorcee, which complicates life for them as well. There remains a stigma on divorcees as being loose women, which can be true if the woman is desperate not to be alone. There are many men who are desperate not to be alone also.

There are many divorced people in church and while many people slander the church of Jesus Christ because there are so many divorced people there, it is actually a good thing that these people are there, because it is right that he or she find the compassion of people in a loving church. It is a shameful thing for the church to turn away the bruised and battered, the hurting and torn, the wounded and impoverished people of society. The church should be a place of healing and shelter from the storms of life.

I am compelled to write about healing from divorce because divorce injures people severely. Sometimes it seems to be the only way out of horrible, abusive situations; this is why the Bible says, "The Lord God of Israel says that He hates divorce, for it covers one's garments with violence . . ." (Malachi 2:16). Divorce hurts people severely. There are good Divorce Recovery groups out there. Because I lived on the fringes of the church for so long, I never went to one when I was first divorced, not after I was told to leave the church I attended. I was given the left foot of fellowship (kicked out) by my church because I got a divorce from my abusive husband. This was a severe wound in my life. My church turned their back on me. The associate pastor was trying to help me, but the senior pastor is the one who kicked me out. It was a liberal church as I was not yet saved. It was a great hindrance to the Gospel in my life.

Twenty years after my first divorce, I went to the Divorce Recovery program at my current church. I had just joined my church at that time. I committed to ten weeks and fulfilled those ten weeks. Interestingly, though I had been divorced twice, I could only deal with my first divorce right then. I had so much anger, bitterness, and even rage inside that it took the entire time to heal from that one, but I did heal. I left it behind in the dust. I had felt such a deep sense of betrayal, but I have healed.

Two years later, I took a course in seminary about what a Christian home is supposed to be like. It made me so sad to know that I had so missed the mark when raising my children. I began to deal with the second divorce at that time. It was an interesting phenomenon. I cried many tears and raged aloud in my car. I yelled, screamed, and vented my frustration when alone, never in front of another person. I wrote in my journal and did everything I knew to do to get out all that toxic emotion.

I talked about the divorce in therapy and let out all the emotion I had held for the twelve years at the time. I knew I could never move on with life until I dealt with the divorce from my second husband. I understood what I did not want in a mate and the next few months would be seeking what I did want in a mate. I began the course in January and it was to end in May, and while the course was designed to teach pastoral people to counsel those with marital difficulties, it was personally like my second Divorce Recovery class. Since I had already dealt with my divorce from my first husband, I concentrated completely on my second. I learned much about what a Christian marriage looks like and what I desired and could expect in the future.

On April 13 of that semester, 2007, my second husband died of throat cancer. I cried and grieved. I did not know that he was deathly ill so it came as a complete shock. I was thankful that my stepdaughter had thought enough of me to tell me and invite me to the funeral. At the funeral, she told me how much I had meant to her when she was growing up and how she knew how I had tried to save her from the hard life she lived as a child. Prior to the funeral, I had thought she must surely hate me, but what a gift she gave me to confirm me in this wonderful way. I cannot imagine why God allowed this death to occur during the time I was struggling to deal with my past hurts by that man. At the funeral, his best friend spoke to me, saying, "He really loved you, he really did. You can believe it." His statement helped me tremendously to go on and to understand how alcoholism is a disease and not something I should take as personal rejection.

The day I returned from the funeral, I got a telephone call saying I had been approved to go on the South American Amazon trip with my church. The church did not know about the death until after I returned from the funeral, so it was a real God-thing. I say this term many times, because many things cannot be explained except to say it is a God-thing. Preparing for the South American mission got my mind off my grief.

I went to the cemetery and placed a stone of remembrance there beside my ex-husband's grave. I cried, sang, and wrote poetry beside his grave. I spent hours there pondering my life and the next course in life I would take. I dealt with all my regrets and my extreme disappointment that he never got his life together and came back to me. I had told him if he would ever truly stop drinking and get right with God that I would take him back in a heartbeat. He never came back. He was too proud to give in to my desires, which he saw as demands, even though he said how much he loved me. His wounds ran too deep in his soul. I did not know how to help him, which grieved me to no end. I began to understand the disease of alcoholism in a deeper way and wanted to help someone with that disease if I could. I found I have not been able to so far in my ministry life, though I tried hard, but the pain in me was too great. He had deep wounds from his childhood that he could not seem to face or deal with.

I must say how much support I received from the seminary class and professor during my time of grief. I received many prayers and thoughtful comments from classmates as I made my ex-husband's death public in the class. I testified how much divorce hurts people, no matter who files the papers and what a devil's trap it really is for people. I received much healing from the kindness and compassion shown me from that group of future ministers. I believe that is one reason God put me in the seminary with pastors and future pastors. He not only is teaching me how to be a good "pastor," but also has shown me many good pastors, as well. I had known so many bad, wicked pastors in my life that, in this new life of mine, God graced me with knowing many good people, pastors, and professors. God is faithful.

We returned from the Amazon about five weeks after my ex-husband's death and it was at that time I realized I was over his death. I had grieved him at the time of the divorce; this was the completion of that grief. I knew in my heart that God forgave me for the divorce and that I was free to move on with my life. I had peace, as I had never known. It was a new beginning for me with life, with my church, and with new friends. I got very comfortable in my new church. I had been in the church for two years, but still felt it was new because I had lived on the fringes there again, except for that Divorce Recovery class. Now I began to truly trust. I was able to use many of my nursing skills on that trip to minister to my teammates. We were all sick, very sick on that trip. I was able to minister to them even though I was also sick. It was very rewarding to me to serve in that way.

After a year of praying and seeking God, I went to speak to my pastor about the possibility of remarriage, asking his opinion of me remarrying. He was the one who ordained me into the ministry and had become a spiritual dad to me; I wanted to honor him and I wanted to honor God. We talked about it and he asked the reasons for my previous divorces, which were adultery, abandonment, and attempted murder (the worst sort of abandonment). My pastor knew my repentant heart and that I had intentionally stayed single for thirteen years at that point because I wanted to be sure if I remarried I would honor God in that marriage. He affirmed that God would honor a marriage commitment for me; I was thrilled.

I went out with one man a couple of months later, a businessperson from a neighboring town. All was going well. He was a Christian and we began to study the Word of God together. However, he had only been divorced a short time and had much healing yet to do. He broke it off with me after four and a half months, which crushed me at the time. He did a bait and switch on me. He reeled me in with talk of Christian marriage, and then dropped me with barely a word. I had really thought he was the one. I would have married him had he asked, but I can see he saved us both a lot of heartache.

I moved on from him and within a short time, I met a man who was a missionary in Africa, a missionary man. This seemed like the ultimate dream of my life, what more could I ask than to be a missionary woman married to a career missionary man? It was what I had always wanted – I thought. Well, I found out what more I could ask. He made it clear to me that he wanted a wife of convenience to raise his six-year-old son because his wife had passed away four years before. He said that, since I had raised two sons, he thought I could handle "the job." It was like a job interview when we got down to real conversation about marriage.

He was not invested at all in the relationship, he wanted no intimacy in marriage. I could not handle that. He was disappointed that he had not found a woman to raise his son. He had bought an airline ticket for me to meet him in his hometown here in the U.S. three states away, because he was home on furlough. I could have loved him had he really pursued me. He then returned to Africa wifeless.

I am so very glad I held out for romance and true love. I went out with my future husband two months after I broke off the relationship with the missionary man. I discovered what I really wanted out of life. I had known my future husband for four years at church, ever since I had joined the church. He is a faithful man of God. One day, God opened my eyes and I "saw" him for the first time! He was so shy, but I told him how I felt about him and the rest is history, wonderful history. We found we both have a love of the outdoors, of adventure, and of living an active healthy lifestyle as long as possible in life. He proposed to me in front of a group of people at church, the choir that we both participated in, got down on his knee, proposed, and offered me the most beautiful engagement ring I have ever seen. I was amazed and astounded.

We married a few months later in a fairy tale wedding even though we were both 50 years old. He had never married before because he was holding out for a Christian woman he could trust. He had desired marriage for many years. The wedding was perfect and then he took me on a honeymoon cruise. I never expected such a gift; I never even desired it because I never thought such a good thing would ever happen to me.

Now I have a fine Christian husband. We have our struggles in marriage as everyone does, but we are fully committed to our marriage covenant, the covenant between the two of us and God. We have had many struggles due to his never having lived with anyone else in his adult life. He always lived alone after he left his parents' home. I had been on my own doing my own thing for the past fifteen years so, and had become set in my ways, as well. We are together and every difficulty we have seems to draw us closer.

I had to have neck surgery within six months of our marriage. I really thought all my neck problems were over after the first surgery, but no. I had had my second neck surgery a year almost to the day of the first surgery. We had to contend with this very early in our marriage. I healed, though it was a much more painful surgery than the first. We have had difficulty with other family members trying to tell us what to do and a host of other inconveniences, but this is the way we see our troubles: as mere inconveniences.

The good life is real. I am an ordained minister, having a doctorate degree from seminary, having ministered as a hospital chaplain, and now minister as an evangelist. I look to a bright future of joy with my husband. He is like no man I have ever been with before. I did not know such a man existed. I am a blessed woman. The entire struggle I went through to heal from DID was so very worth it all to get to the place that I now am in life. I am tremendously happy. Never give up hope, my dear friend. Life is so worth living, even if it does not seem like it now. For me, years passed before I believed life to be worth living. I am so glad I persevered; God made it all worthwhile and has restored my life in an even better way than it was previously. He is a faithful and amazing God. Here is a fairy tale written as an allegory of my life.

A Fairy Tale

Once upon a time, there was a young princess, Princess Camilla of the Kingdom of the Dark Hinterlands, an evil Land of Long Ago. Though she was princess of the Dark Land, she rebelled and fought against the evil forces of that wicked kingdom. Her heart was filled with Hope, a thing quite foreign to the land of her childhood. She had been stolen from the Land of Hope at birth by foreigners from the wicked Kingdom of the Dark Hinterlands. She was filled with craven fear sometimes, but in her heart had been placed a warrior spirit, a fierce constitution that dared to Hope, but from whence it came, she knew not. Her very name meant "warrior maiden," her birth name. This warrior spirit gave strength to her fight when she needed it most, at those times when she felt helpless, afraid, and tormented. She never felt that she belonged anywhere, and of course, did not remember that she had been stolen from her native land. She was told she was owned by and indebted to the royalty of the Dark Hinterlands and such it would always be. She lived in the Royal Palace of Darkness, a lonely and wretched place surrounded on all sides with dark woods.

There lived an evil troll in the Woods of the Way Back, way back in the caves of the Hinterlands. He stayed under the Bridge of Evil Dreams, taunting passers-by. The bridge was the only way into the caves of the Dark Hinterlands. Though she was a princess, she was given grueling tasks to do by cruel taskmasters who did not treat her like a princess at all. Why did they treat her this way? What had she done wrong? But such is the way of the Kingdom of the Hinterlands.

One day, she thought she had found her prince of Hope, but he was in actuality the evil troll disguised in clothes of goodness and light. Verily, the people of the palace gave her to this disguised imposter and she soon found herself to be in the Land of Forgotten Hope and No Love. She had heard the voice of the one she thought to be her kind prince who would rescue her, but he had deceived her greatly and proved to be very cruel and punishing. He carried her away to the caves of the Dark Hinterlands; there she lived in fear and torment, and dreamed of being rescued by some benevolent soul. Even the Palace of Darkness seemed better than the dark caves. She would hide from him every chance she got.

There were, then, two young princes well loved by their mother, Princess Camilla. In what seemed to be a futile task at times, she perpetuated the fight for Hope. A force greater than she gave strength to her fight, though she knew not the Source of that strength. She desperately tried to give this strange idea – Hope – to her young princes. A young mother, the princess loved the young princes with an unconditional love, unending love – very strange in the land of the evil kingdom. She dreamed of running far, far away with her young princes. However, she knew the evil troll would always find her and punish her all the more.

As the princess went about her daily chores, heavily burdened under the weight, she had to come out of her hiding place and walk across the Bridge of Evil Dreams where the evil troll stayed most of the time, frightening anyone who would dare to cross, especially her. Many times a week she had to cross and the evil troll taunted and threatened her always. "See here, Miss Princess, whose princess do you think you are? I will take the princes from you and kill you and feed your carcass to the wild beasts!" She had to hear this every time she traveled across that bridge on her daily journeys, and his words kept her up at night away from the Land of Peaceful Dreams. These threats frightened her, but she did not fear them too deeply, sometimes . . . but sometimes she did.

Then one day, her worst fear came upon her. The princes were stolen away by the evil troll! Unthinkable! Too young to leave their mother, they had no choice! They had to work under the bridge with the evil troll and live among his people way back in the caves of the Hinterlands, while she was forced out of the caves, running for her very life, left to wander in the Land of Faraway Places. In those caves, the princes took on the ways of, and came to resemble, the evil troll and his people. They lost their princely ways, but merely for a time, she trusted.

When the young princes were stolen away, Princess Camilla searched for them high and low until she discovered what had happened to them, how they were tricked into following the evil troll to live deeper in the caves. Where was Hope then? After that, Princess Camilla traveled far and wide seeking she knew not what. She grieved in her heart almost to her death. In her anguish and despair, she searched. She traveled to the Land of Faraway Places many times in her quest for the "Unknown." Her quest was not fruitless for it ended in her discovering the Land of Hope Again, a lovely land with lots of gardens, a land of abundant provision, a friendly place full of love and nurture. She heard of the King of the Land of Hope Again Who ruled in His Kingdom of Light and hoped in her heart of hearts that He was real and if so that He would want her to be His somehow, not knowing she truly belonged to this

Kingdom from birth. She dared to Hope, but sometimes, alas, she doubted that she was worthy of love and affection, acceptance and belonging. She sometimes doubted this seemingly elusive Hope of hers as well. The Land of Darkness had deceived her innocent heart.

Princess Camilla had heard that the King had promised that one day He would come for those who wanted to be His, the Hope of Love, and that they would truly be His. She believed. She called to Him, "Please O great King, please take me in if You would. There would be nothing greater than to be with You, O King!"

The King heard her cries and came for her! She learned that the King had been the Source of her strength all along and that no one could come into His Presence without hearing the call that He sent out, His very Word. She had just wanted to be His, to belong to Him. Princess Camilla heard the call of the King and He accepted her just as she was: rejected and unloved, wounded and heartbroken. He began to heal her broken heart and granted her a home with Him forever! Hope was rekindled!

The Hope of Love, the King himself, took her in. The Good King took her to live in her rightful Kingdom, the Kingdom of Light in the Land of Hope Again, and she gladly worked for Him because she loved him. "His yoke was easy; His burden was light" (Matthew 11: 30). No more hard taskmasters were to torment her in this new Kingdom! She gladly followed the King. She could not believe at first that this was really happening to her, that the King was truly real, that He was good, and that He would allow her to do His work, which gave her life meaning and purpose. She could not believe at first that He was her Father and she was His child. Then she did believe and came to know a Love that she had never known before – ever. Hope was poured into her once-broken heart. Hope became real to her. She found that she had a reason to live – because the King lives!

Princess Camilla became royalty in the House of her Father, King Abba. She lived under the protection of her Warrior King. King Abba gave to her a portion of His Warrior Spirit and this spirit rose in her again as in the days of her youth. At last, she knew the Source of her strength! However, working for Him meant that she had to journey across the mountain, and way deep in the valley back to the Hinterlands many times to rescue those who also had been stolen away at birth yet truly belonged to the King. The task meant danger, but He promised to go with her always. Did she mind the danger? No, she did not because she loved the King, and besides, He went with her everywhere she went.

The princess never forgot the young princes who, to her, would always be princes. She was happy that she could be nearer to them when she went across the mountain and deep into the valley. She did her best to send messages to them in the caves to win them over to the ways of King Abba, of the Kingdom of Light. One day, she did get her message through to them, and the evil troll was exceedingly angry and filled with fury. She feared, as had become so natural for her, but then she remembered whom she really belonged to, that He was right beside her, and she had Hope Again.

Princess Camilla got word to the young princes that she wanted them to meet this glorious King. They told her that they came to meet Him and that they would follow His ways, but follow, they did not. It was because the ways of the evil troll and his people were rooted deeply within their wounded souls. This broke the princess' heart, but she never gave up on them throughout her whole life. She loved them with unconditional love always, forever and ever. She trusted the King always to watch over them. After some time, the princes came to trust in the King, which pleased Princess Camilla so very much.

Trust was difficult for Princess Camilla, even after she came into her rightful Kingdom as princess, for she had been deceived so many times. However, she learned that the people of King Abba's Court can be trusted, those who are truly His people. As she journeyed forward in her new life, King Abba sent many of His Kingdom's choicest servants to encourage her heart and teach her His ways. There were, however, some evil trolls disguised as His servants, as "People of the Kingdom," deceiving her if they could. She learned she must stay close to the King to hear Him whisper, "That one's not mine, but that one is. You can trust that one!" She found she must stay close to hear Him, to hear His heartbeat. The Kingdom was in her heart all along and that is where she heard her Father, the King Who lives in the Ever After.

By and by, Princess Camilla came to know, really know, that she belonged to the King and would forever be in His Kingdom of Light, that she was His true child, a true princess. Glorious as this newfound kingdom of hers was, she longed for a true prince to hold, a prince to be with in this life, knowing that it would be some time before she could follow her King into the Ever After. She had many suitors along her way, met many imposters, but still she seeks the one who can be her faithful love in her lifetime in the Here and Now. Will she find him? Does he exist? Will she journey on alone? She would continue to be a lonely sojourner in this land if her King wanted her to. Only the King knows. Will He tell her ?

Six months later . . .

Many suitors and imposters came and went along the journey, but none could satisfy the longing for true love in the heart of the fair Princess Camilla. She began to learn to hear the King more often to know when an imposter showed up. She knew deep in her heart of hearts, however, that her King who loved her would bring her intended handsome prince for her to love in the Here And Now. And that is just what the faithful King did. He had promised and she had believed Him. Faithful is He!

Prince Christian rode into her life, dressed in white, riding on his white steed, and took her away with him where he lived, also near the King. The King Himself gave Prince Christian, a true son of the King, to her in a quite remarkable and surprising way! The prince had been there very near to her for a good long time, though she did not recognize him as her own. The King was preparing her for him with the beauty treatments, as He did for Queen Esther of long ago.

Before her appearing, Prince Christian had waited and waited for word from the King that his princess had been given to him. He began to doubt and lost Hope; yea verily, his Hope was gone. He had lost heart and had begun to stray into the Land of Forgotten Hope and No Love where the princess had once lived, but a powerful Force restrained him. He knew he belonged to the King, though he did not understand His divine plan. But Prince Christian's heart was true to his King and he continually served Him even when he thought his King had forgotten the desires of his heart. However, the King had not forgotten and kept the prince close in His care. He had a surprise plan for the prince's good and true happiness, which included this new princess who would be his.

One day, the King opened Princess Camilla's eyes to see the handsome prince's face – thrice she saw his face and dared to hope for her love in the Here and Now. Her King whispered in her ear, "Look, he's the one! I will show you that he can be trusted and you shall no more be ashamed. He will forever cause you to forget the evil ones with their evil deeds done against you. Together you will be fulfilling each other's dreams, yet will be finally fulfilled in Me, your King. Your prince will love you as I do. You have learned that you can trust Me, child, now trust him, take his hand and give him yours. You are both in My House now where good things happen. He will be your family in the Here And Now and you will ride on together doing My will into the Forever And Always." She obeyed her King, trusting in His goodness, and Prince Christian returned to the Land of Hope Again, this time with his princess by his side.

Prince Christian and Princess Camilla were perfect for each other, something that only their good King could arrange. He had made their dreams come true. They were so very happy together serving Him, singing His praise, and worshipping His Person. And they lived happily ever after and dwelt in the Land of Hope Again forever and always.

The End.

🙢🙠

This fairy tale is not a mere fairy tale; however, because it is a fairy tale that came true! The two had a fairy tale wedding and are living happily ever after.

Well, I know that marriage is not a fairy tale, and this is the real world, but this is a childhood dream of mine that I never expected to happen to me because I expected nothing good to come from my life. God has His wonderful surprises and knows what we all want even when we do not, for a time. "Delight yourself also in the Lord; And He shall give you the desires of your heart" (Psalm 37:4).

My husband and I love travel and physical activities, such as camping, hiking, and backpacking, even though I've had spinal surgeries. I intentionally did not marry a man in ministry. Men I was in relationship with had taunted me and degraded my intelligence. I got very tired of this type of man telling me that I was stupid or not intelligent enough to understand spiritual matters. I wanted a man who would love me just as I am and for whom I could do the same. I made the right choice this time.

The need for surgeries on my neck, several herniated discs requiring hardware placement and fusions, were caused by all the abuse I had given my body over the years working as a nurse and ignoring the pain. The discs were pressing into my spinal cord and causing softness in the cord. The surgeon, who I trust completely due to his reputation, told me if I did not have the surgery I was facing a wheelchair soon and then a life of being bedridden. I could not stand the thought of that and agreed to the surgery. I had to have a second surgery because my body did not completely heal, but now my spine is well stabilized, though there had been much pain. I now have hardware in the front of my neck and the back of my neck stabilizing the neck securely. I am thankful for the pain being in the past and am truly enjoying life now.

My husband is God's gift to me; we know that God put us together for a reason and it is to our great delight. We love each other. As one of my favorite verses says, "Every good gift and every perfect gift is from above, and comes down from the Father of lights, with whom there is no variation or shadow of turning" (James 1:17).

It is my sincere prayer that every reader out there will find peace and joy in his or her life and a partner with whom to share life. Fight for your healing, set your boundaries, do not let abusive people hurt you any longer; forgive those who have hurt you. When the abusers begin their abusive stuff, simply walk away or hang up the phone. You can do it! It is true freedom. New life is glorious.

I have found relief from my troubled life and it is my sincere prayer that you will find relief as well. I believe that you can find relief and achieve a new life. God can overcome even the most horrendous troubles. I have no doubt that others have life stories that are far more traumatic than mine, but this is not about comparison. Do not think that your life story does not count because it seems little to you; if it affected your life it is by no means little. If it seems too high a mountain to climb, believe me, with God it is not. My purpose is that your personal story will no longer hold power over you, no matter what it is, and that it will not control you for the remainder of your life. It does not matter your age, whether you are fifteen years old, or less, or ninety years old, or more. There is never a wrong time to work this work. Hope happens. It takes daring and boldness, but you can do the work. The rewards are truly tremendous and exciting. Please do not be as some who stay stuck in addictions and mental illness hiding and covering their pain all their life. Step out and test the waters. If you start to sink, take the hand of Jesus; He will lift you.

A graduate student at a university in Asia asked me in recent years, "What is most precious thing to you in life?" My immediate response to her was, "Jesus Christ!" I meant this with all my heart. I then sang a song to the small group of Asian students declaring my love to Him. I just do not sing by myself in public, but did that day in that class. It was God's grace. He has given me His amazing grace, is forever faithful, and has guided and provided for me. He has loved and kept me, and will keep my soul forever. I owe Him everything. My Father loves me. I am "Abijah," which means, "God is my Father." I ask my Lord to help me stop all wrong motives for doing His work on earth.

I entitle the next section, "I Relinquish All the Junk." I relinquish that I once built my life upon my self-righteousness, and the self-life. I relinquish my attempts at being some great minister, being a great nurse, or a great anything, and my career, as I know it. I relinquish getting all my family saved (to come around to my way of thinking and not just to believe the Word of God, the Bible), saving the world as a penance to God, how prideful I was, trying to validate my existence on earth when all my worth is in Christ. I relinquish my anger and bitterness at what was done to me, rage, revenge, and venomous talk and thoughts concerning my parents, particularly my mother, my dad, my exes, my ex in-laws, and anyone who stood in the way of my children and me. I relinquish control.

I relinquish my suicidal and homicidal thoughts, all mental illness, my pain, my victim mentality, and the two greats of my life – guilt and shame. I relinquish all the curses against me by others and the ones I repeated to myself all through the years, as well as the ones I made up along the way. I forgive all the people that cursed me and I forgive myself for perpetuating those curses and making new ones. I relinquish unforgiveness now and forever.

I relinquish all helplessness, hopelessness, depression, and anxiety, anything that holds my energy level back and keeps me from enjoying life. I give up the desire for the American Dream, as I know it. I will continue to live, and, now with my new husband, I will enjoy things in life I never knew before.

I relinquish all my expectations that were never met, all my disappointments in life, the things in life I will never have, like my dad's acceptance and the belief that all my family will change overnight. I relinquish my rights to my own life and give all my life over to my Lord Jesus Christ.

Furthermore, I relinquish self-abuse, self-abusive talk, self-flagellation, self-centeredness, selfishness and demanding my own way, fear that caused me to try to control people in my life and/or be the captain of my own life, and the fear of losing control. I relinquish the fear of going crazy, losing my mind for good, the belief that I have been crazy and stupid; I relinquish and give it all up. I have built my life on many bad things as well as good things, all in an effort to validate my existence and intrinsic self-worth as a human being, trying to obtain what was already mine in Christ.

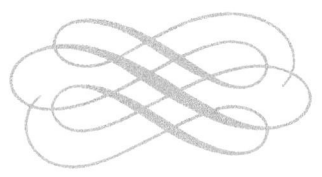

CHAPTER 11

MOVING ON

So then just as you received Jesus Christ as Lord, continue to live
your lives in Him, rooted and built up in Him, strengthened in
the faith as you were taught and overflowing with thankfulness.
(Col 2: 6-7).

Being confident of this, that He who began a good work in you
will carry it on to completion until the day of Jesus Christ.
(Phil 1:6).

You have dwelt long enough at this mountain;
turn and take your journey.
(Deuteronomy 1:6-7) (NKJV).

You have stayed long enough at this
mountain; break camp and move on.
(Deuteronomy 1:6-7) (GNB).

Where will I go from here? I will keep doing what I am doing
now, ministering to as many people as I can and worshipping
in my church with my husband; only God knows the next step. He
gives only enough light at our feet to see the next step: "Your word

is a lamp to my feet and a light to my path" (Psalm 119:105). On the path of life, He shows us the next step in His light. He has never led me astray. I am fully confident in His ability to "keep me by the power of God through faith" (1 Peter 1:5). This pertains to faith in the name of God, of Jesus Christ.

Jesus said, "I am the Light of the world, he who follows Me shall not walk in darkness, but have the light of life" (John 8:12). I have found the Light; rather He has found me. My pilgrimage is finding Jesus Christ and of the truth of my past. Persons have asked me now at the end, "Was it worth it to go through all the work that you had to go through to get here?" My answer is a most definite, "Yes!"

The facts remain, earthquakes happen, tornadoes happen, people die, children are abused, bad things happen to good people, signifying "tribulation in this world" (John 16: 33) as stated, but I believe in God to keep me through all the tribulation and to give me peace in the midst of it all. He has proven Himself faithful too many times to count. There is a biblical promise that states, "The Lord has appeared of old to me saying, 'Yes I have loved you with an everlasting love. Therefore with loving kindness I have drawn you'" (Jeremiah 31:3). God's love draws us toward Him. He does the work if we will allow Him.

We do learn service from the Master, service to God and man. The way we serve God is to serve others out of our love for God. What we do, we do out of love and devotion to the Lord Jesus. We must obey, but it is the most joyful obedience ever, for, "You will show me the path of life; In Your presence is fullness of joy; At Your right hand are pleasures forevermore" (Psalm 16:11). Just being with Him is exhilarating pleasure! Yes, we must obey what He has said in His Word, and this is what stops so many. Now, hearing the term "obey," people may say, "I don't want to obey anyone or anything. I do my own thing!" My question to you is this: does your life work as you have been living and doing your own thing? If not, it could be time for change—yes, the C word – change! God is our Maker and our Maker knows us inside and out. He is able, willing, and eager to take care of us in every single aspect of our lives, and the joy is "inexpressible and full of glory" (1 Peter 1:8).

Even now I have begun to enjoy life so much I feel it cannot be true. I have tied up some loose threads of my life and am working on others. I have written new poems to reflect changes made in the most recent past, poems of healing and wonder at God's great creation. I have written these pieces while on trips away from home with my husband, in the midst of the beauty of God's creation. These thoughts reflect my life's current theme of "breaking camp and moving on" (Deuteronomy 1:6-7).

Voices in the Wild

a cacophony of voices
eeking through the trees
whistling softly southward
in the pines, the aspen leaves

peacefulness reigns here
nature, intrepid in this place
what absence of fear, what peace, what rest
peace transcends time and space

many sights, many voices
whispering winds speak nomenclatures
shades of green, shades of brown
unforgiving nature

beautiful destroyers
growing over oak and maple leaves
their beauty is deceitful
killing as they thru the foliage weave

mindless of human weakness
nature rages, nature roars

birds of prey and the eye of the eagle
far above the forest soar

God's beauteous creation
how can all this just be?
no accident or evolved progression
just look, a Masterful creation I see!

Words About Life

losing a loved one gaining one
too romantic love
friendship love
unconditional love
called agape
celebrating all seasons
so many words have been written
to express a thousand petals of flowers
a thousand autumn leaves
a thousand snowflakes
a thousand butterfly wings
the beauty of mountains
the beauty of oceans and rivers,
of streams, of brooks
a baby's first cry
a baby's coo
first words
and paradoxically
last breath at end of life
words about hatred and strife
the sting of separation
injustice and war
murder and mayhem

mystery and danger
the shadow of death
the harshness of life
the ways of the world
the human condition
good and evil,
is there nothing?
is there nothing unexpressed
by a song, a poem, a book, a legend,
a tale or a memoir?
I imagine there is absolutely nothing

I wrote the words to a song, which a friend of mine wrote music to; her name is Megan Grace Fowler. She did a great job with the music; here are the words.

Abba Love

Relentless love
Love so relentless and never ending
True and sure in a world so torn
Inclined to you His ear is bending
He loved you before the day you were born.

Chorus: Abba Love with give you a reframe
Abba will give you a new name
Abba Love takes you through the war
Abba tells you who you are
We all need Abba Love
Relentless Love Abba Love
We all need God's true love
Relentless Love Abba Love

Love so sweet and so pure
Ever far-reaching

Like sprinkles of mercy and blooms of grace
The world of pain His love is breaching
Mercy triumphs in each broken place.

Bridge: No more will you be called rejected
           Abba delights in you
           He's always accepted you child
           Abba makes all things new
           Through belief we receive Abba Love

Yeah relentless love
Love so relentless oh Abba's Love

The following is the poem I have needed to write about my Mama. The words mark closure to the troubled portion of my life. My heart is healed as I write about the good memories of my childhood when I had previously thought that none existed. In my poem, my words may not seem much to the outside observer, but these memories were pearls of great significance to me. I bask in the glow of each word and the memories they radiate. I no longer idealize Mama as a perfect person; however, the good in her will always remain in me and has shaped my view of the world. I was able to mother my own children lovingly because of her love.

Mama

these are the sights, sounds, and scents
of motherly childhood love
pearls, white gloves, and red rouge
expensive perfumed powder
real nylon stockings with garters
squeaky little voice singing lullabies at night
reading me storybooks and telling me stories

as she sat in her special chair crocheting
antacid tablets in a purse too long
soft pink robe and warm pink blanket
warmth and freedom from fear when she was near
nurture and refuge from the night
love and acceptance most days
prim and proper
proud and spiritual
little gifts, like the little fish
Christmas morn delights

On the path of my healing journey, I now have hope for my future whatever that may be.

My husband and I love tent camping and hiking still, and both keep in good shape for our age. We both know if we slow down too much that our momentum may be lost. We are more realistic about life, about love, and about how we minister for the Lord Jesus Christ. It could happen one day that we will no longer camp in a tent, but in an RV. Our appearance will probably be different than one might envision us to look.

I am moving on in life, in ministry, in church, and always with the Lord Jesus Christ. My husband and I love to minister together, and now that he is retired from his long-time job, we are free to travel the U.S. and beyond. He and I travel to do mission work to give testimony to how Christ has worked in our lives and to take His hope and His love to others. We have overcome our major obstacles emotionally and spiritually. We know that we need God in order to be able to minister to others' needs. We know the importance of taking care of ourselves. We plan to hike the Appalachian Trail in the next few years. We are goal-setters and find that if we set specific goals, we are likely to complete them.

Hope was the key and Faith unlocked the Door [Jesus]
All the children are together now living completely free
The Door is wide open forevermore
And I never gave up on me!

This is my prayer for you as well, that whatever path you are on, you will find healing hope and strength to work to get well and whole. Also, that you will never give up on you! Hope is real. It is wonderful to live and want to live. My continued hope and prayer is that you will also find healing and the desire to live life to the fullest. Scripture states, "But to you who fear [reverence] My [God's] name, the Sun of Righteousness shall arise with healing in His wings; and you shall go out and grow . . ." (Malachi 4:2). My healing is a gift from God and has been an amazing adventure.

God is so good at foiling the enemy's plans for our life. He redeems lives. What Satan sent to destroy, God turned it around for my good and ultimately His good. Satan's plan was to kill me long ago, but God had other plans. I was scarred in childhood and young adulthood. I believe the scars remain, though the power that made those scars is broken. The Bible tells me to "Seek good and not evil" (Amos 5:14), and that is what I will do. Here is one final devotional poem before I close. "To Him [God] be glory forever and ever. Amen!" (2 Timothy 4:18b).

My Poem

My poem is my peace
My one heart joy
That grows like a flourishing tree
My Guide, my Glory
And the Lifter of my head
When God speaks, He meets each need!

My poem is my faith
My one heart grace

That flows from Living Water
You are my Peace
My reason to believe
That You are my Abba Father!

My poem is my life blood
My one heartbeat
That flows from the heart of the Lamb The
Lamb that was slain rose again
Won't you meet Him
He's the great I Am!

My poem is my call
My one heart sound
That's found in the cleft of the Rock
In the still quiet place
Not in fire or earthquake
I hear my sweet Lord talk!

My poem is my prayer
my one heart song
that comes on the wings of a Dove
the manna that comes from Your dear heart
that assures me that You are Love.

My poem is my song
My one heart cry
That comes on healing wings
In distant lands
My sweet Lord told me
"It's not time to die, but sing!"

My poem is my name
My one heart identity
That threatened my life and health

Fight I have done
And now I have won
I take care of all of myself

My poem is my shout
My one heart praise
That's meant for only One
My Lord took my place
And bought me by Grace
I cry, quickly Lord Jesus please come!

EPILOGUE

My healing pilgrimage began at my conversion to Jesus Christ in September 1995. God directed me to enter Bible College in Dallas, Texas. At the onset of college, I found a church to go to that helped with my diagnosis of DID by leading me to Christian psychologists. There I found help in 1997 from a female therapist that I met with for about one year. She then quit to be a stay-at-home mom to her children. After this, in the year 2000, I met with Ray and have seen him ever since, some 24 years later. He has helped me immensely. I say I could not have done it without him, but he says I could not have done it without myself helping myself by doing the difficult work of therapy. It is hard but rewarding work to get well, it is so worth it. God is my steady Guide. This I know, I could not have survived this work without God guiding me into His Truth.

I am an RN, a psychiatric RN. I understand what my patients are dealing with, and it is very rewarding to me. I have done this type of work for 10 years, while having been a nurse a total of 45 years. I have always worked. I began at age 15 and still work. But I am a working person that found a great God! My life moves on. I am an ordinary person, an everyday person who always wanted to do something great for God. I tried and will try. I am reminded of the quote by William Carey, the great missionary, and I try to live my life by it. It is, "Expect great things from God, attempt great things for God." I have received great things from God. I stayed in

Bible College for some years until I entered seminary in 2005. My motivation for going to seminary was to learn more about my God and His ways.

My husband Randy and I got married in 2009, which was a dream come true for me. I never expected to marry again (see Chapter on Mission Journeys). He has been a Godsend in my life, the love of my life. God put us together no doubt. He is very supportive of the call of God on my life to go on mission. I am very thankful for him. I am not an easy person to live with or be around sometimes and yet he puts up with me. He is amazing. Yes, we are a normal couple and have many heated discussions at times, particularly about money but we survive together and only want to be together. He is supportive of me in my mental health as well.

In 2013, I went to a physician in town that had me see his nurse practitioner. I only had the diagnoses, which were already overwhelming to me of: Major Depressive Disorder, DID, PTSD, and anxiety disorder. This nurse practitioner marked on my chart that I am Bipolar. The physician came along and agreed with that diagnosis next time I saw him. I was furious when I found out. I did not find out until 2018 or 2019 when I obtained a copy of my doctor's office chart. It was a devastating blow. Even my psychiatrist had not diagnosed me that way.

Looking back with all things factored in, it makes perfect sense. I have had problems with relationships, handling money, feeling suicidal at times, being tempted to do petty theft, manic behavior – really in my case I would get angry and rage (it was never a good feeling or productive time with me as with some people who love Bipolar for the reason of great productivity during manic times; I have never stayed up for days in that way), and was very talkative at times being loud and silly. I had racing thoughts and could not quiet my mind to sleep sometimes. I got myself in physically dangerous situations intentionally and believed myself to be safe in those situations. I was plagued with mood swings and instability in my work life, in marriage and family, and socially. I was afraid of people and kept myself isolated much of the time. This has been a lifelong push in my life, to keep myself isolated because I could not trust others. I was in a profession where I ministered to the needs of others, but in my downtime, I kept to myself. I went into the ministry as well, but still had trouble socially on my own time.

In my marriage with my godly husband, I would fly into a rage at times early in our marriage. I would yell and scream at him, completely out of control. I had homicidal thoughts at times and suicidal thoughts at other times due to old baggage and ways of thinking. God kept me by His Grace. He keeps me every day and makes me victorious in my life. I now am living a good life. There were many things that I had to ask my husband's forgiveness for; he always forgave me. My mood is now stable due to medications and having had much talk therapy along with pastoral counseling. But awhile ago, in December 2022, I had a complete shift in thought about therapy.

I was graduating from seminary with my doctorate in ministry degree and was spending time in prayer. I was thinking about the future and how God might use me with my new degree. I wondered if I had a purpose for doing it or if I had just done it for myself. It was not an easy thing to accomplish. It was difficult and it was very emotional in doing everything I had to do for the degree so now I know it was not just for myself. But I had no idea what my next step should be. The Holy Spirit quickened to me what I had been told in one of my first seminary courses, Pastoral Ministry. My professor oversaw biblical counseling at Southwestern Baptist Theological Seminary. I had been told that God's Word is sufficient for all human problems.

I believe that the Word of God is true and is fully inerrant. I believe in the scriptures that speak of God's power being manifest through the Word but did not understand anything about biblical counseling. I thought that the biblical counselors were hard on people and told people they just need to believe more, and they would be all well. Well, I had been told this but not by biblical counselors. Pastoral counselors and ministry leaders had told me this. I imagined that this was the way of biblical counseling. I imagined that these counselors were simply people that would not take the time for people's needs. Now I believe this can be true but I have determined not to be this way with people. I am learning of the love of God and patience that is needed to do biblical counseling. I also thought they might tell mentally ill people not to take medications, but this is not the case.

I had originally thought after spending five years as a hospital chaplain that this was to be my course. But it is not to be as hospital chaplaincy has proven to be antithetical to my evangelism ministry. I did not evangelize in the hospital setting because I was taught not to, but I have found that even my Christian beliefs are said to be wrong for chaplaincy. To me, it seems they do not want anyone to believe anything Christian. I was told I was cold and judgmental, not open to other opinions or spiritual beliefs yet this was just not true. They want chaplains who are inclusive of other beliefs even in their own lives. I have learned that, at least in my area, that this is not for me. I am in biblical counseling at SWBTS studying for certification. We do not always get what we want in God's plan but what we get is the absolute best for us. First, I wanted to be a full-time missionary, but now know that I would have come home in defeat due to my problems with my mental health. Second, I wanted to be a hospital chaplain. It seemed the best plan for someone who has been a hospital RN for 45 years. It seemed logical. But God directed me to biblical counseling, and I know that He knows best for me. I am so happy doing this type of counseling and full of joy when I am studying. I will minister as an imperfect person, a wounded healer.

I know in my heart that Bipolar is not the end of the line for me. I do know the life implications though. Jesus is my Healer. If he chooses to heal me in this life I will be thrilled and thankful. But if he chooses not to, I will always praise Jesus and worship him alone. I will always seek to serve Jesus and others. This is what makes life livable and gives purpose to it. Jesus said, "I am the way, the truth, and the life. No one comes to the Father except through me" (John 14:6). Jesus is our hope, our joy, our peace, our life and love. He is the purpose-giver giving us a reason to live.

I will take medication for my issue unless Jesus chooses to heal me, which I know is possible. I continue to take the medicine because I know that I can live a normal life if I do. Persons who stop taking medications and begin to drink and drug end up in the hospital. I do not want to go there. So, I take meds and stay completely away from alcohol and drugs. I also stay away from these because I want to be healthy and because the Lord wants me to be a good steward in taking care of my physical body. When I was seventeen years of age to age twenty, I smoked marijuana, drank alcohol, and took pills attempting to shut off my inner turmoil. When I began nursing school, I completely stopped all illegal drug use. I wanted a life of service to others, a clean life.

I still want a life of service to others. But to do this, I will need to talk about these issues and disorders I have in my life. This is not palatable; this is not fair. I struggle with feeling abnormal and like an orphaned child, unloved and unwanted. I know that I need to be strong in my resolve in order to be used by God. God and I have business to attend to in prayer before I am finally free. The Allender book that I am reading calls me to struggle and wrestle with God over my story basically until I love it. At this point, I cannot imagine loving my story. It is one of abuse, neglect, heartache. How can I love my story? I do not know yet. I am to be thankful for the rain.[40] Metaphorically, rain is the bad stuff. Embrace the bad stuff? I must be thankful for the bad stuff. I believe this quote, "As we see our story used for his glory, we are disposed to love what has been written for us to live."[41] I just continue to pray, "Lord, thank you for keeping me alive and for loving me and causing me to feel loved. Help me through until I love my story." Love mental illness? I do not know about this. But I know where my hope comes from.

We have hope, the anchor of our souls. Hope is Jesus. Jesus is the anchor of our souls. He is also peace, the Prince of Peace (Isa 9:6). There is no arguing with our creator God, to do so is to forfeit

---

[40] Dan Allender, *To Be Told: Know Your Future, Shape Your Future.* (Colorado Springs: Water Brook Press, 2005), 179.
[41] Ibid., 180.

our peace. To have the "peace that passes understanding" (Phil 4:7), we must surrender our lives to God, choose to obey His lordship, repent of our sins, and basic to all this is to be born-again (John 3:3). We can be born-again by turning ourselves, our whole lives over to Christ, believe his work for us on the cross, and believe he is God. "Confess with your mouth the Lord Jesus and believe in your heart that God raised him from the dead, you will be saved" (Rom 10:9).

I am working hard on being more social with my church group. It meant going where I could not be anonymous; I had to get to know people. I really did not want to do that, but I did. For a long time, I would simply not go to Sunday school because I figured if those people knew me, they would either hate me or ridicule me. I had quite a paradigm shift. I have had to fight to remain in community at church. Jesus comforts my heart and is teaching me when people are safe. I am in community at church. I am beginning to know that I am accepted and cared for there. It is easier than it was once.

My parents were not emotional and never said "I love you" to each other and to anyone else that I know about. Not long ago, God began to give me scriptures to say how much He loves me and wanted me to be born. The most fearful verse in the Bible to me is "Depart from me, I never knew you!" (Matt 7:23). This next verse answers this verse and begins the most comforting three verses in the Bible to me. First, "Before I formed you in the womb, I knew you; before you were born, I sanctified you; I ordained you a prophet to the nations" (Jer 1:5). Second, "For you formed me in my mother's womb. I will praise You for I am fearfully and wonderfully made, marvelous are Your works. And that my soul knows very well" (Psalm 139: 13-14). And third, "But as many as received Him, to them He gave the right to become children of God, to those who believe in His name, who were born, not of blood, nor of the will of the flesh, nor of the will of man, but of God" (John 1:12-13). My Father God wanted me. I was born by His will. I am so very thankful that He is mine and that I am His. I cannot express in words the depth of these truths and the joy they bring me.

As a child, I had no voice to defend myself. I am finding my voice even today. I can write my feelings, my story of my past, present, and future, but to speak these out is a different issue. I was silenced in my childhood and youth, never being allowed to talk back to my parents or ever stand up for myself. This was true for all of us in my family, not just me. All efforts were labeled defiance. I was not a defiant child, but just wanted to be free to speak. After I went to college and Bible College, I found some of my voice. In seminary, I reclaimed more of my voice.

As for the future, ministry is my goal. Biblical Counseling will be my ministry as well as evangelism as I have been doing it. I want to take the Gospel of Christ to the hurting as well as give my testimony. I want others to become worshippers of our great God. I want to teach new converts how to worship and know our Lord. I want to see others healed by the power of God. I want to be involved in missions throughout the world. I also have this "other life" of being with my husband who wants to work and not retire. He has one more year until he must retire, however. I want to go with my husband traveling across the United States as a tourist because he wants to do this. I have no problem with what my husband wants to do, but I confess I do not know how it will all play out. I love my husband and my ordinary life. I never thought I wanted "ordinary," but always I wanted "normal." So, I have it now. I began writing my story, the story written herein in 2010. I have revised it again and again.

In conclusion, this is my story and I embrace it. It has not been easy to embrace, but it is necessary to do so. I realize that my story can cause others to say, "She's just crazy." There is quite a stigma on mental illness, but I am shameless in this. I sent my story out anyway. It does not matter anymore what people think. The story I must tell is between God and me. I have overcome some things and still deal with some things in the scope of mental illness, but I am not defeated.

I am first and foremost a child of God committed to Jesus Christ my Lord for life. I want my story to be used for God's glory. I deeply desire to help others along their way. There are many forgotten and wayward children of God living with mental illness. It does not have to be that way. There are so many people living with mental illness and the population is quite forgotten and stigmatized. I wish to change all that and will do what I can in my little corner of the world with everything I have in me. I am not walking alone, but God is with me. He is Hope personified.

"This I recall to my mind; therefore, I have hope. Through the Lord's mercies we are not consumed, because His compassions fail not. They are new every morning. Great is Your faithfulness. The Lord is my portion, says my soul, therefore I hope in Him!" (Lam 3:21-24).

"My flesh and my heart may fail, but God is the strength of my heart and my portion forever" (Psalm 73:26).

RESOURCES

Allender, Dan. *To Be Told: Know Your Story, Shape Your Future*. Colorado Springs: Waterbrook Press, 2005.

_____. *The Wounded Heart*. Colorado Springs: Nav Press, 1990.

_____ and Tremper Longman III. *The Cry of the Soul*. Colorado Springs: Nav Press, 1994.

Bass, E., and L. Davis. *The Courage to Heal: A Guide for Women Survivors of Child Sexual Abuse* (4th ed.) New York: William Morrow Paperbacks, 2008.

Chu, J.A. *Rebuilding Shattered Lives: Treating Complex PTSD and Dissociative Disorders* (2nd ed.) Hoboken, NJ: John Wiley and Sons, 2011.

Cowman, Charles Mrs. *Streams in the Desert*. Grand Rapids: Zondervan Publishing House. 1925.

Diagnostic and Statistical Manual of Mental Disorders, 5th Edition, DSM-5. *Bipolar*, 2013.

Diagnostic and Statistical Manual of Mental Disorders, 4th Edition, DSM-IV. *Dissociative Fugue*, 1994.

Gil, Eliana. *Outgrowing the Pain: A Book for and About Adults Abused as Children*. New York: Dell Publishing, 1983.

Gingrich, Heather Davediuk. *Restoring the Shattered Self: A Christian Counselor's Guide to Complex Trauma*. Downers Grove, IL: IVP, 2013.

Hubbard, M. Gay. *More Than an Aspirin: A Christian Perspective on Pain and Suffering*. Grand Rapids: Discovery House Publishers, 2009.

Lewis, C.S. *Mere Christianity.* New York: Macmillan Publishing. 1952.
_____ *The Chronicles of Narnia: The Lion, The Witch, and The Wardrobe.* New York: Harper/Collins Publishers. 1978.

Mitchell, Jeffrey T. PhD, C.T.S. *CISM: Group Crisis Intervention 4th Edition.* Ellicot City, MD: I.C.I.S.F., Inc. 2006.

Nouwen, Henri. *The Wounded Healer.* New York: Doubleday, 1990.

Oksana, Chrystine. *Safe Passage to Healing: A Guide for Survivors of Ritual Abuse.* New York: Harper Perennial. 1994.

Pearlman, Laurie Ann, and Christine Courtois. *Relational Treatment of Complex Trauma,* Journal of Traumatic Stress, Vol. 18, No. 5, October 2005.

Piper, John, and Justin Taylor. *Suffering and the Sovereignty of God.* Wheaton, IL: Crossway, 2006.

Priolo, Lou, *People Pleasing.* Phillipsburg, NJ: P and R Publishing Company, 2007.

Ross, Colin. *Dissociative Identity Disorder: Diagnosis, Clinical Features, and Treatment of Multiple Personality.* New York: John Wiley and Sons, Inc. 1997.

St. John of the Cross. *Dark Night of the Soul.* Poem written between 1577-1579.

The Fifth Dimension. *The Age of Aquarius* album. Recorded by Soul City Records for the musical, *Hair.* 1969.

The New Strong's Concordance/Vine's Dictionary of the Bible. Nashville: Thomas Nelson Publishers. 1999.

Tolkien, J.R.R. *The Hobbit: or There and Back Again.* London: George Allen and Unwin Ltd. of London. 1937.

Tracy, Celestia G. *Mending the Soul Workbook for Men and Women.* Phoenix, AZ. Mending the Soul Ministries, Inc., 2015.

Tracy, S.R. *Mending the Soul: Understanding and Healing Abuse.* Grand Rapids: Zondervan, 2005.

Webster's Dictionary 1987 Edition. Miami: P.S.I. & Associates, Inc.

Sidran Institute

Coffey, Rebecca. *Unspeakable Truths and Happy Endings: Human Cruelty and the New Trauma Therapy.* Sidran Institute Press, 1999.

Cohen, Barry, Esther Giller, and Lynn W., eds. *Multiple Personality Disorder from the Inside Out.* Sidran Institute Press. 1991.

Downing, Rachel, LCSW-C. *Understanding Integration as a Natural Part of Trauma Recovery.* Sidran Institute Press.

Giller, Esther. *The Effects of DID on Children of Trauma Survivors.* Sidran Institute Press.

_____. *What is Psychological Trauma?* Sidran Institute Press.

_____. *How to Choose a Therapist for Post-Traumatic Stress and Dissociative* Conditions. Sidran Institute Press.

Jennings, Ann PhD. *Retraumatizing the Victim.* Sidran Institute Press.

Lewis, Lisa PhD., Kay Kelly MSW, LSCSW, and Jon G. Allen PhD. *Restoring Hope and Trust: An Illustrated Guide to Mastering Trauma.* Sidran Institute Press.

Mason, Patience Editor and Publisher. Sidran Institute Press.

What are Traumatic Memories? Sidran Institute Press.

What is Dissociative Disorder? Sidran Institute Press.

What is PTSD? Sidran Institute Press.

Wilkerson, Jennifer. *The Essence of Being Real: Relational Peer Support for Men and Women Who Have Experienced Trauma.* Sidran Institute Press.

Websites

American Psychiatric Association: http://www.psych.org. Accessed 1/10/20.

DSM-IV. *Dissociative Fugue.* http://www.cme.psychiatryonline.org. Accessed 5/12/20.

Mayo Clinic: *Dissociative Identity Disorder.* http://www.mayoclinic. com. Accessed 12/2/19.

Mayo Clinic. *Major Depressive Disorder.* www.mayoclinic.com. Accessed 3/15/20.

Mental Help Online. *Types of Stressors (Eustress vs. Distress).* http:// www.mentalhelp.net. Accessed 5/13/20.

Psycom: http://www.psycom.net. Accessed 12/2/19.

Sareen, Jitender MD, FRCPC. *Post-traumatic Stress Disorder in Adults: Impact, Comorbidity, Risk Factors, and Treatment.* http://www.ncbi.nlm.nih.gov. Accessed 5/13/20.

Substance Abuse and Mental Health Services Administration. www.SAMHSA.gov. Accessed 3/17/2024.

The Merck Manual Online. *Depersonalization/Derealization Disorder* http://www.merckmanuals.com.. Accessed 5/13/20.

The Merck Manuals Online Medical Library on *Dissociative Fugue*: http://www.merck.com. Accessed 5/1/20.

Web M.D. on *Dissociative Identity Disorder.* http://www.webmd.com. Accessed 5/11/20.

www.ingramcontent.com/pod-product-compliance
Lightning Source LLC
Chambersburg PA
CBHW071328120626
46546CB00002B/489